AMERICA

ALSO BY FERNANDO VALVERDE

The Insistence of Harm

ALSO BY CAROLYN FORCHÉ

In the Lateness of the World

What You Have Heard Is True: A Memoir of Witness and Resistance

Blue Hour

The Angel of History

The Country between Us

Gathering the Tribes

AMERICA
FERNANDO VALVERDE

**TRANSLATED AND WITH AN INTRODUCTION
BY CAROLYN FORCHÉ**

COPPER CANYON PRESS

PORT TOWNSEND, WASHINGTON

Cover art: Robert Frank, *U.S. 285, New Mexico,* 1955; copyright by Andrea Frank
Foundation, from *The Americans*

Copper Canyon Press is in residence at Fort Worden State Park
in Port Townsend, Washington, under the auspices of Centrum.
Centrum is a gathering place for artists and creative thinkers from
around the world, students of all ages and backgrounds, and
audiences seeking extraordinary cultural enrichment.

LIBRARY OF CONGRESS CATALOGING-IN-PUBLICATION DATA

Names: Valverde, Fernando, 1980- author. | Forché, Carolyn, translator,
    writer of introduction. | Valverde, Fernando, 1980- América. |
    Valverde, Fernando, 1980- América. English.
Title: America / Fernando Valverde ; translated and with an introduction by
    Carolyn Forché.
Description: Port Townsend, Washington : Copper Canyon Press, [2021] |
    Summary: "Fernando Valverde is widely regarded as one of the most important
    younger Spanish-language poets. Here his vibrant voice and convictions are
    translated and introduced by Carolyn Forché, herself a world-renowned poet"
    —Provided by publisher.
Identifiers: LCCN 2021025539 | ISBN 9781556596223 (paperback)
Subjects: LCSH: Valverde, Fernando, 1980---Translations into English. |
    United States--Poetry. | LCGFT: Poetry.
Classification: LCC PQ6722.A58 A8313 2021 | DDC 861/.7—dc23
LC record available at https://lccn.loc.gov/2021025539

9 8 7 6 5 4 3 2

COPPER CANYON PRESS

Post Office Box 271
Port Townsend, Washington 98368
www.coppercanyonpress.org

Acknowledgments

America is for Nieves García Prados because we discovered it together. Without her the nights would be a dark place populated with wolves.

This book would not have been possible without the first person who believed in me in the USA, the poet and translator Gordon E. McNeer, who is the central person in *America* because he is a central person in my life.

During my seven years in the United States I have met wonderful people to whom I have to give thanks for many reasons:

Thanks to Carolyn Forché, for her translation and for her friendship.

Thanks to Karen Stolley and to David Littlefield, my family in Atlanta.

Thanks to Clyde and to Kim, for William Carlos Williams.

Thanks to Allen Josephs, for being a home in Florida and in the Mediterranean.

Thanks to Tony Geist, who always had a hug ready for healing.

Thanks to Fernando Operé, because he saved me from the abyss on a train trip to NY.

Thanks to Jericho Brown, my brother, my friend, my hope.

Thanks to Axel Presas and Blanca Catalina Garcia and their princesses, Valentina and Gaia, who are magical.

Thanks to Natasha Trethewey, for joining hands with me, for her way of loving me.

Thanks to Ilya Kaminsky for the poetry, for what we share.

Thanks to Donald Hall, who opened the doors of his home to me.

Thanks to Harold Bloom and to Pedro Larrea for that unforgettable lunch.

Thanks to Robert Hass for our walks through Bogotá, for his unbeatable advice.

Thanks to Tracy K. Smith, the first to send this book to a publisher.

Thanks to Robert Goddard for our Friday afternoons.

Thanks to Charles Simic for cooking for us, for opening his Balkan home to us in New England.

Thanks to Rita Dove, mentor and inspiration, light when there's a shortage of air. And to Fred, a smile that speaks a thousand words.

Thanks to James Byrne, because his letters always make me feel at home.

Thanks to Irene Gómez Castellano and to Luis Correa, a resting place along the way, many unmentionable secrets.

Thanks to Ross Null, master gunsmith, who graciously introduced me to the guns used in the "Shootings" section of this book.

Thanks to Juan Felipe Herrera, *mi gitano mágico*.

Thanks to Yusef Komunyakaa, for walking beside me by the graves of sorrow.

Thanks to Raúl Zurita and Paulina for our *vida rompiéndose*.

Finally, thanks to all of you who came to my assistance in a country in which sometimes I was a stranger, in which at other times I felt at home, and in which for the most part I had the sensation of being on an endless voyage: Miguel Valladares-Llata, Paula Sprague, Gustavo and Karen Pellón, David Gies, Ricardo Padrón, Michael Gerli, Andrew Anderson, Sam Amago, Mané Lagos and Randolph Pope, Nauzet Lozano Alvarado, Nathalie Handal, Andrea Cote, Jeremy Paden, Michael Marling de Cuellar, Don Pangilinan, Laura Wood, Katie Rice, Shawn Harris, Federico Díaz-Granados, José Sarria, Alicia López-Operé, Allison Bigelow, and Isaac Mbiti . . . And thanks to the one who was always on the other side of the Atlantic to give me a comforting word, to bring my world close to me: Remedios Sánchez.

To exchange Spain for America caused me to lose many things. I could wind up like in that poem by Alberti, "What I Left, for You." Unfortunately, what is lost is gone forever. There was no American Dream. There was no gold in those hills. But on my way through the forests and on the highways of America I met all these people who offered me relief.

To Nieves

Y así volvimos a nuestro lugar, estos Reinos,
pero ya sin la paz, en este viejo régimen,
con un pueblo extranjero aferrado a sus dioses.

We returned to our places, these Kingdoms,
But no longer at ease here, in the old dispensation,
With an alien people clutching their gods.

T.S. Eliot

ÍNDICE / CONTENTS

SHOOTINGS

LA TIERRA SALVAJE / THE WILD LAND

INTRODUCTION

I FIRST ENCOUNTERED THE WORK OF FERNANDO VALVERDE at the Congreso Internacional de Poesía y Poética in Puebla, Mexico, in 2016. The auditorium that night was filled, so I stood in the back to experience the frisson of this rare literary event for Puebla: a reading by Valverde, whose vibrant, incantatory, lyric art is regarded as among the finest produced by the new generation of poets writing in Spanish. He had, two years earlier, been nominated for a Latin Grammy for his collaboration with flamenco musician Juan Pinilla. Poet Alí Calderón of Mexico urged me to meet him, as did Colombian poet Federico Díaz-Granados. Together with Raquel Lanseros of Spain and Francisco Ruiz Udiel of Nicaragua, these poets were building a pan-Hispanic poetry movement, reaching across oceans and continents to enliven poetic art in their common language. Although Valverde is from Europe and not the Americas, he is considered vital to the project.

Later in the festival, we met and talked, and so began a friendship, with further meetings at festivals in Bogotá, Colombia, and his natal city of Granada, Spain. He was already living in the United States, where he had begun an unusual pilgrimage: to visit as many sites of mass shootings as he could, to walk through the scenes of these horrific crimes, to talk to survivors, to study the perpetrators, and even to fire the weapons they used—to experience what it felt like to fire them. He was on a singular mission, in some respects resembling one undertaken by another poet from Granada almost a century earlier: Federico García Lorca, who visited New York City during the Great Depression and would go on to write *Poet in New York*, arguably his greatest work.

"Lorca arrived the year of the stock market crash and found what he believed to be the end of capitalism," Valverde told me during one of our conversations. "His stay was brief. His book was always on my mind, because Lorca's is the epitome of Spanish poetry, and because I'm from Granada. Lorca wanted to write the drama of capitalism. I have preferred to talk about America, what it means today, the tension between the best and the worst."

Another difference from Lorca is that Valverde feels indebted to Latin American poets: Pablo Neruda, César Vallejo, Vicente Huidobro, Ernesto Cardenal, Claribel Alegría, and Raúl Zurita. And Valverde acknowledges a deep admiration for English-language poets, beginning with the Romantics, then Walt Whitman and Emily Dickinson, and the work of the living Americans he has met, among them Natasha Trethewey, Jericho Brown, Ilya Kaminsky, and Tracy K. Smith. To write his *America*, he says, "it was necessary to abandon the rhythms of Spanish, and to compose within [his] own language an American music."

On his travels in the United States, nothing amazed him so much as gun violence. He finds it ironic that the first modern mass shooter was a man named Charles Whitman: "One Whitman created the symbolic image of America and another Whitman fired at it." This happened shortly after the Kennedy assassination, Valverde said. "In 1966, Charles Whitman climbed the tower of the University of Texas at Austin and began shooting, opening an abyss in the word *America*. Charles Whitman had left behind a letter asking the scientific community to study his brain because he could not control his hateful thoughts. In the autopsy, they found a brain tumor. So who pulled the trigger? The weapon was fired by Whitman, but maybe not through his will."

Valverde traveled extensively in America but didn't want to write "touristic" poetry, and he hoped not to exhibit naiveté regarding violence, however much it shocked him. He journeyed as deeply into the country as he could. A few days after the mass shooting at First Baptist Church in Sutherland Springs, Texas, he was there, talking to survivors and praying for the victims at the scene of the massacre. Valverde had worked for a decade as a foreign correspondent for *El País,* reporting from the Balkans and the Middle East, but here he was no longer limited by journalistic constraints and could dispense with any pretense of dispassionate objectivity. Valverde was acquiring knowledge through immersion, with the hope that it might be possible to make of what he felt and of what he saw a poetry that achieved the transformative, whether his subject was personal or social, private or public.

Just as he was struck by the coincidence of the two Whitmans, he was also attentive to the substrate of myth, the persistence of self-delusion, and the denial of complicity that characterize the particular consciousness produced by the American experiment. As a European poet resident in the United States, he has endeavored to know his adopted country by visiting the graves, cultural shrines, cities, and—most especially—crime scenes having to do with the country's history of enslavement, poverty, addiction, and mass murder. His itinerary included Fulton Avenue, Baltimore; Camden, New Jersey; Walt Whitman's tomb; Ellis Island; Savannah, Georgia; the banks of the Mississippi; Wyoming State Penitentiary; Route 66; and the northern ports of New England. Through lists and accountings in the enumerative mode, in biblical cadences and with Whitmanesque vision, *America* connects our perilous present to our country's genocidal and settler-colonial foundation, established at the speed of rapacious capitalism. Valverde considers white men overtaken by their rage, men who "keep to themselves," "lone wolves," suicides who fear going to death alone, whose country permits amassing weapons of war, in the service of killing civilians in Columbine High School, Virginia Tech, the Westroads Mall, Sandy Hook Elementary School, the Pulse nightclub in Orlando, Mandalay Bay hotel in Las Vegas, and the aforementioned First Baptist Church in Sutherland Springs. In *America,* we visit all of these sites.

Along with Jack Kerouac, the musicians Kurt Cobain and Jeff Buckley also appear, the former leaving behind his cigar box of heroin works, the latter drowning in the Mississippi while swimming fully clothed. The Buckley poem riffs on Leonard Cohen's "Hallelujah," an imaginary soundtrack for the fatal swim. Cobain's cigar box becomes an emblem of doom. The first shooter, Charles Whitman, is joined by the revenants of others: Lee Harvey Oswald, James Earl Ray, Sirhan Bishara Sirhan, and Mark David Chapman, most of them now American ghosts. But Valverde's mosaic of the country is also grouted with admiration and love: an elegiac poem for Donald Hall, whom he visited at Eagle Pond farm, and one for his friend Natasha Trethewey in memory of her mother.

When he asked me to be the translator of *America*, I realized that the work of assimilating another poet's sensibility, of musical transposition, and of discerning linguistic equivalence and tropic resonance would be complicated by the strange experience of regarding my country and culture from the other side of the mirror. It is the vision of someone looking back from a reflection he has, himself, produced. This was, for me, a challenging and intriguing prospect, and because I already felt such affinity with Valverde, I was honored to accept. The result is the *America* you hold in your hands.

Carolyn Forché

Note: *America* here is written without the accent over the *e* to signify that we are referring to the United States and not to the whole of the Américas.

AMERICA

Los hijos del emperador celebran la abundancia unidos por lo que ya no existe

Allí comerás y te saciarás

Deuteronomio 8:10

En vil mercado convertido el mundo

Espronceda

Cuatrocientos mil muchachos muertos para liberar al mundo,
las aguas de los ríos se llenaron de sangre,
las aguas de los ríos de Europa con sangre de America
fluyendo por el Danubio y el Sena,
peces muertos y hedor irrespirable en la ribera del Rin,
en los puentes del Támesis.

Cuatrocientos mil muchachos muertos son el futuro
convertido en serpiente
frente a los ojos del profeta,
a este lado del muro queda la libertad,
el mundo libre
nacido de la victoria
de los muchachos muertos.

Las aguas de los ríos volvieron a calmar la sed,
fue limpiada la sangre de los baldes de madera
y de las piedras y de las montañas,
y en las casas florecieron las cocinas,
y los edificios se levantaron
unos encima de otros
como escaleras de emergencia
y la soledad fue un caminante dentro de la multitud,
y la muchedumbre una sombra detrás de la abundancia,
y entonces de los ríos emergieron millones de ranas

The Sons of the Emperor Celebrate Abundance at One with What No Longer Exists

When thou hast eaten and art full

Deuteronomy 8:10

The world turned a vile marketplace

Espronceda

400,000 children killed to free the world,
the waters of the rivers filled with blood,
the waters of the rivers of Europe with the blood of America
flowing through the Danube and the Seine,
dead fish and an unbreathable stench on the banks of the Rhine,
on the bridges of the Thames.

400,000 dead children are the future
become a serpent
before the eyes of the prophet,
on this side of the wall there is freedom,
the free world
born of the victory
of the dead soldiers.

The waters of the rivers quenched thirst again,
washed the blood from the wooden ships
and the stones and the mountains,
and in the houses kitchens flourished,
and the buildings rose
one on top of the other
like fire escapes,
and solitude was a wanderer within the multitude,
and the crowd a shadow chasing abundance,
and then millions of frogs emerged from the rivers

que poblaron las cocinas y los hornos y las artesas,
y el polvo de la tierra se convirtió en piojos
sobre las bestias y los hombres,
y bandadas de moscas llenaron las casas de los avaros,
pero tampoco esto fue suficiente,
el frío sembrado en el corazón
siguió trepando
hasta convertirse en peste
peste
moviéndose como un huracán por las grandes llanuras,
el hambre tiene el sabor de la carne podrida,
el infierno era una sala de fundición,
cadenas de montaje,
la avaricia no entiende las razones de la patria,
la avaricia circula con libertad,
atraviesa los muros, las fronteras, las divisas, los cálculos,
tienes que recordar que esta tierra no es tuya,
tienes que recordarlo,
repite una y otra vez el emperador,
porque lo peor está por llegar,
lo peor no fueron los últimos cincuenta mil muchachos muertos
que llenaron de sangre el río Saigón,
el mal está en la sangre de los que llegan
al infierno de las fundiciones,
unidos por lo que ya no existe.

Ellos serán las úlceras sobre los cuerpos
de los hombres y de las bestias,
sólo la piedra podrá proteger los frutos y las raíces,
sólo la piedra podrá servir como resguardo.

Llegaron huracanes,
tornados,
raciones de comida al amanecer,

that filled the kitchens and the ovens and the troughs,
and the dust of the earth became lice
on beasts and men,
and swarms of flies filled the houses of the misers,
but this, too, was not enough,
the cold sown in their hearts
kept rising
until it became a plague

moving like a hurricane through the great plains,
hunger had the taste of rotten flesh,
hell was a foundry,
assembly lines,
greed does not understand the justification for a fatherland,
greed circulates freely,
it crosses walls, borders, currencies, calculations,
you have to remember that this land is not yours,
you have to remember it,
the emperor repeats again and again,
because the worst is yet to come,
the worst was not the last 50,000 dead children
that filled the Saigon River with blood,
the evil is in the blood of those who arrive
in the hell of the foundries,
united by what no longer exists.

They will be the boils on the bodies
of man and beast,
only stone will be able to protect fruit and root,
only stone can serve as a shelter.

Hurricanes arrived,
tornadoes,
food rations at daybreak,

fuego mezclado con granizo
desgajando los árboles,
destrozando los muros y los diques del emperador
para inundar las casas de quienes sufren.

Pero el corazón del hombre que ocupaba la casa dorada
        permaneció helado,
porque de nada sirve mostrar la fuerza del viento y de la tempestad
a quienes nunca fueron
alivio en el fracaso,
a quienes no supieron lo que significa
ser la derrota por la indiferencia,
ser agua antes que sangre.

Y el barro fue la culpa pegado a los zapatos de los caminantes,
fue la sospecha y también la vigilancia,
pestillos en los portones,
razones de seguridad,
arcos de detección de metales en los aeropuertos,
deportaciones masivas y nuevas leyes
para calmar el miedo a la libertad.

Una vez que los hijos quedaron insensibles
a la dureza del emperador,
a la avaricia,
al vil mercado,
a los códigos escritos con el dolor de los débiles,
cuando todos dejaron de prestar atención
acostumbrados a la solemnidad,
protegidos detrás de las palabras y de la corrección
y de las cuentas corrientes
y de la propaganda
y de los argumentos que desmienten la propaganda,
todo estaba ya listo para la llegada de las más densas tinieblas

fire mixed with hail
tearing the trees,
destroying the walls and dikes of the emperor
to flood the homes of those who suffer.

But the heart of the man who lived in the golden house
                remained frozen,
because the force of the wind and the storm was useless
to those who never experienced
relief from disaster,
to those who did not know what it means
to be defeated by indifference,
to be water before blood.

And guilt was mud stuck to the shoes of those who walked,
it was suspicion and also vigilance,
latches on the gates
for safety reasons,
metal detectors in airports,
mass deportations and new laws
to calm the fear of freedom.

Once the children became insensitive
to the hardness of the emperor,
to greed,
to the vile market,
to the codes written with the pain of the weak,
when everyone stopped paying attention,
accustomed to solemnity,
protected behind words and correctness
and bank accounts
and propaganda
and arguments that belie propaganda,
everything was ready for the arrival of the thickest darkness

en las que nadie pudo ver a su prójimo:
sólo el bastón dorado del emperador
era reconocible para todos,
sólo en sus manos estaban ya los hombres y las bestias
y también las mujeres
y las langostas
y los campos arrasados por las langostas.

El final es conocido y antiguo,
la muerte de todos los primogénitos,
ya se tratara del hijo de un emperador
o de un preso
o de una bestia.

Y no hubo casa alguna en la que no se helase el corazón de
        los hombres.

in which no one could see his neighbor:
only the golden staff of the emperor
was recognizable by all,
now only in his hands were men and animals
and also women
and locusts
and fields razed by locusts.

The end is known and ancient,
the death of all the firstborn,
whether the son of an emperor
or a servant
or a beast.

And there was no house in which the hearts of men did not turn
        to ice.

Los condenados de Fulton Avenue persiguen las señales del cielo y de la tierra

Por encima del suelo se elevan las señales,
cables de los que cuelgan la ruina o el porvenir,
todos los imprecisos sentimientos
sin disciplina
como en una emboscada en la que espera
la enfermedad
con sus labios
quemados.

La vida de los hombres sucede en las señales,
porque las casas fueron clausuradas,
tapiadas
puertas y ventanas
selladas
llagas
lámparas
de cristal.

La calle transporta negros muertos hasta las esquinas,
donde esperan beber la leche de la resurrección
que se reparte en bolsas o en papel de aluminio.

Estar en posesión
del fruto de la amapola
o del hielo o la tiza
se paga con la cárcel.

Estar en posesión
con la visión borrosa
y la euforia
y las alucinaciones
campanas que doblan como gemidos

The Condemned of Fulton Avenue Follow the Signals from
Heaven and Earth

Above the ground they hang
from wires, a sign, the ruins or the future,
all the vague feelings
without discipline
as in an ambush in which
sickness awaits
with its burning
lips.

The life of these men happens in the signs,
because the houses were closed,
boarded
doors and windows
sealed off
open wounds
street-
lamps.

The street moves dead Black people to the corners,
where they hope to drink the milk of the resurrection
that is distributed in packets or aluminum foil.

Being in possession
of the fruit of the poppy
or ice or chalk,
one pays with jail.

Being in possession
of blurred vision
and euphoria
and hallucinations,
bells that groan rather than toll

justo antes de las náuseas,
es la condena.

La sed.
En las esquinas
venden botellas de agua en oferta
los camellos
vigilan
junto a los proxenetas
Fulton Avenue
con Lexington,
las escaleras de incendios son un atajo al cielo,
las escaleras que bajan al sótano
están llenas de calambres
en la oscuridad,
moonshine por las rendijas de las tablas en las ventanas,
la historia de la libertad escrita en madera podrida.

La vida de los hombres sucede,
la de las mujeres también
sucede
una
y
otra
vez
con el ruido que hace la esperanza
al estrellarse,
con las súplicas
y el zumbido de las avispas
sobre las manzanas
mordiendo
los pezones
de las jeringuillas.

just before nausea,
is a condemnation.

Thirst.
On the corners
they sell bottled water cheap
the dealers
watch
together with the pimps
Fulton Avenue
and Lexington,
fire escapes are a shortcut to heaven,
stairs that go down to the basement
are filled with cramps
in the dark,
moonshine through the slits of boarded windows,
the history of freedom written in rotten wood.

The life of men happens,
that of women too
happens
and
again
and again
with the sound that gives hope
when crashing,
with supplications
and the hum of wasps
among the apples
sucking
the nipples
of syringes.

La sed.
La sed de America
sonríe satisfecha a la muerte,
sin pulso ni voluntad.

Thirst.
The thirst of America
a smile satisfied to death,
without pulse or will.

Los muchachos de Camden

Nadie podrá explicarles que hay que dejarlo todo
        para la inmortalidad.

Hoy son hombres del norte,
los que tragan el polvo y escupen sobre el cemento.

Hoy he podido verlos llorando como niños.

Muchachos que trabajan en talleres cerca del cementerio de Harleigh,
hombres y mujeres vestidos de domingo que entran en la catedral,
que entregan sus cuerpos igual que abren las puertas de sus casas,
Cordero de Dios que quitas el pecado del mundo,
son lo que llaman pueblo, son la miseria
que se agrupa y que siempre acaba dentro de los ataúdes,
son también la lujuria, el ruido que les impide escuchar,
son los hijos de los hijos de la esclavitud.

Los escucho reír a carcajadas sobre los cadáveres,
los escucho cantar, aunque son mudos,
me siento a contemplarlos en la esquina de la 4ª
        con Martin Luther King Boulevard
y siento lástima, y hartazgo,
y también hastío,
yo que he abandonado los lugares que más amaba,
que he visto en sueños llorar a mi madre sin motivo,
siento lástima y culpa porque voy a abandonarlos,
y ellos lo saben,
pueden verlo en mis ojos como dos cicatrices,
yo voy a abandonarlos
como he abandonado tantas veces lo que más quería,
podré borrar la culpa de dejarlos en la otra orilla del río Delaware,

The Boys of Camden

No one can explain to them that it all must be left up to immortality.

Today they are men from the north,
those who swallow dust and spit on concrete.

Today I could see them crying like children.

Boys working in shops near Harleigh Cemetery,
men, and women in Sunday dresses entering the cathedral,
who offer up their bodies just like they would open the doors of
        their houses,
Lamb of God that takes away the sin of the world,
they are what you call a people, they are misery
that clusters together and always ends in coffins,
they are also lust, the din that prevents them from listening,
they are the children of the children of slavery.

I hear them laugh out loud about the corpses,
I hear you sing, although you are dumb,
I sit to watch them at the corner of Fourth and Martin Luther
        King Boulevard
and I feel pity, and satiety,
and also disgust,
I have left the places I loved the most,
those I've seen in my dreams where my mother cries for no reason,
I feel pity and guilt because I'm going to abandon them,
and they know it.
You can see it in my eyes as two scars,
I'm going to abandon them
as I have abandoned so many times what I most wanted,
I can erase the guilt of leaving them on the other side of the
        Delaware River,

pero no olvidaré sus pasos vacilantes bajo la lluvia fina,
ni el llanto de mi madre intuyendo el abismo que ahora nos separa.

but I will not forget faltering steps under a fine rain,
nor the cry of my mother sensing the abyss that now lies between us.

La noticia de Dios al otro lado del puente Benjamin Franklin

Todos llevan su cruz y la soportan
sin exageración,
sus espaldas muestran la gravedad,
la curvatura última del universo,
la redención del hombre,
una condena antigua sobre una mano abierta,
pero no van a detenerse aquí,
han llegado al final
y siguen caminando como peces,

Only in God is my soul at rest;
from him comes my salvation.

Ellos llevan
la noticia de Dios por toda la tierra,
Señor del cielo y los océanos,
tú que todo lo escuchas,
llanto y melancolía,
Señor de la nieve y de la lluvia,
tiende tu mano misericordiosa,
llena sus corazones solitarios de amor,
apiádate de estos hombres que caminan,
apiádate de todos los que pagan
un dólar para cruzar el puente Benjamin Franklin,
de todos los que pasan obedientes y respetan
la luz de los semáforos,
la castidad
y la Constitución,
de aquellos que aprendieron
a repetir el coro de tus oraciones
aunque vaguen desnudos después de la ebriedad.

The News of God on the Other Side of the Benjamin Franklin Bridge

All have their crosses to bear and carry them
without exaggeration,
their backs show the gravity,
the ultimate curvature of the universe,
the redemption of man,
an old sentence on an open hand,
but they are not going to stop here,
they have reached the end
and they keep walking like fish,

Only in God is my soul at rest;
from him comes my salvation.

They carry
the news of God throughout the earth,
Lord of the sky and the oceans,
you who listen to everything,
crying and melancholy,
Lord of snow and rain,
extend your merciful hand,
fill their lonely hearts with love,
take pity on these men who walk,
take pity on all those who pay
a dollar to cross the Benjamin Franklin Bridge,
on all those who obey and respect
the light of the traffic signals,
chastity
and the Constitution,
of those who learned
to repeat the chorus of your prayers
even if they wander naked after drunkenness.

Miro el prodigio de las aves,
un niño las observa desde Camden
señala al cielo
mientras se escucha el vértigo de las ambulancias.

También las aves gritan.

I watch the prodigy of the birds,
a child observes them from Camden
points to the sky
while listening to the vertigo of ambulances.

The birds also cry out.

Herida frente a la tumba de Walt Whitman

Tú que viste los vastos océanos
y las cimas de las montañas,
que contemplaste a los marineros del mundo
y viste comer a Cristo el pan de su última cena
      en medio de los muchachos
y de los ancianos,
tú que viste al verdugo de Europa
con su hacha empapada de sangre,
que pisaste el patíbulo
y los campos en los que las madres lloraban a sus hijos muertos.

Dime si todavía
es posible anunciar la justicia triunfante
y entregar las lecciones del nuevo mundo.

Voy a besar tus labios,
están fríos y saben a la palabra *America*.

The Wound before the Tomb of Walt Whitman

You who saw the vast oceans
and the mountain peaks,
who communed with all the sailors of the world,
and you who saw Christ eat the bread of his last supper among
      the young
and the elders,
you who saw the executioner of Europe
with his ax soaked with blood,
you stepped on the scaffold
and the fields in which mothers cried to their dead children.

Tell me if it is still
possible to announce triumphant justice
and deliver the lessons of the New World.

I'm going to kiss your lips,
they are cold and they taste like the word *America*.

LA TIERRA PROMETIDA

THE PROMISED LAND

Deja tu tierra natal y la casa de tu padre, y ve al país
que yo te mostraré. Yo haré de ti una gran nación y te
bendeciré; engrandeceré tu nombre y serás una bendición.
Bendeciré a los que te bendigan y maldeciré al que te
maldiga, y por ti se bendecirán todos los pueblos de
la tierra.

Get thee out of thy country, and from thy kindred, and
from thy father's house, unto a land that I will shew
thee: And I will make of thee a great nation, and I will
bless thee, and make thy name great; and thou shalt be a
blessing: And I will bless them that bless thee, and curse
him that curseth thee: and in thee shall all families of the
earth be blessed.

Genesis 12:1–3

Ellis Island

Ellos han decidido abandonar la tierra,
dejar atrás la casa de su padre y el ataúd cerrado
y el país
donde los recuerdos se pudren.

Han escuchado que la nación
entre todas las naciones,
la bendecida,
aquella cuyo nombre brilla más que ningún otro
porque un día estuvo en los labios de los profetas,
se encuentra al otro lado del océano.

El porvenir
se vende en billetes de primera y de segunda clase
en los puertos de Nápoles,
de Trieste,
de Constantinopla,
crece sobre la bruma de Bremen
o la llovizna de Hamburgo
o la soledad de los muelles de Liverpool.

A la llamada acuden los desposeídos
con sus cuerpos expuestos al frío y los insectos,
con su plegaria tan parecida a una queja
y el escozor,
y el fracaso,
ellos son quienes marchan hacia la tierra prometida
porque la suya les fue arrebatada
o porque cuando nacieron
toda la tierra tenía un propietario
y no encontraron forma de alimentarse
pero sí de reproducirse

Ellis Island

They have decided to abandon the land,
leave behind the father's house and the closed coffin
and the country
where memories rot.

They have heard that the nation
among all the nations,
the blessed one,
whose name shines more than any other
because once it was on the lips of the prophets,
it is found on the other side of the sea.

The future
for sale with first- and second-class tickets
in the ports of Naples,
of Trieste,
of Constantinople,
grows on the haze of Bremen
or the drizzle of Hamburg
or the loneliness of the Liverpool docks.

The dispossessed come to the call
with their bodies exposed to cold and pestilence,
with a prayer so like a complaint,
and the stinging,
and failure,
they are the ones who march toward the promised land
because theirs was taken from them
or because when they were born
the whole earth had an owner
and they did not find a way to feed themselves
but were able to reproduce

en los márgenes de las panaderías
sobre la cubierta de los barcos
en las salas de espera de los hospitales
o en los vertederos
dieron a luz multitudes de bocas y de vientres
para repartir su pobreza
y para ser luego la fuerza de las fábricas
o de los campos de cultivo,
la ideología de los vencedores,
la justificación,
el nombre de la patria y la autoridad de los otros.

La muchedumbre navega hacia los muelles de America
y los alcanza con muy mal aspecto
y hedor
y el miedo agazapado debajo de la esperanza
que es más fértil que el trigo
y puede alzarse sobre los océanos,
crecer en la sequía
o multiplicarse sobre la miseria.

Pero a la tierra prometida no entrarán los débiles ni los enfermos
tampoco los inválidos
porque el pueblo elegido será la raza
que reciba en sus manos el porvenir.

El regreso será el destino de los contagiados
porque la malaria también viaja sobre las cubiertas
y es más fértil que el trigo
como fértil es el tifus de los trópicos,
el cólera del Mediterráneo,
los anquilostomas de la tierra húmeda de Irlanda,
la tiña de Polonia y de Hungría,
el tracoma que crece en las patas de las moscas de Ucrania.

alongside bakeries
on the decks of boats
in the waiting rooms of hospitals
or in landfills
they gave birth to throngs of mouths and bellies
to spread their poverty
and then to become the workforce of the factories
or of fields under cultivation,
the ideology of the victors,
the justification,
the name of the country and the authority of others.

The multitudes sail toward the wharves of America
and reach them looking sickly
and smelling worse,
and fear cowers beneath their hope
which is more fertile than wheat
and can rise over the oceans,
grow in drought
or multiply in times of misery.

But the weak and the sick will not enter the promised land
nor will the invalids
because the chosen people will be the race
that receives the future into its hands.

The infected are destined to return
because malaria too travels over the decks
and it is more fertile than wheat
as fertile as the typhus of the tropics,
the cholera of the Mediterranean,
the hookworms of the damp earth of Ireland,
the ringworm of Poland and Hungary,
the trachoma that grows on the legs of Ukrainian flies.

La tierra prometida no será un reino para los ciegos
ni para los enfermos mentales
ni para quienes se nieguen a desnudarse
porque llevan el dinero cosido a la ropa
por miedo.

Nada tiene que ver con la avaricia,
el precio de la libertad es la eterna vigilancia.

Dios bendiga a los hombres que alcanzaron la tierra
de la libertad.

Dios bendiga a los hombres elegidos
para la gran cosecha del futuro.

The promised land will not be a kingdom for the blind
nor for the mentally ill
nor for those who refuse to undress
because they carry their money stitched to their clothes
out of fear.

It has nothing to do with greed,
the price of freedom is eternal vigilance.

God bless the men who reached the land
of freedom.

God bless the men chosen
for the great harvest of the future.

Esclavos de Guinea llegan a la plantación de Buenaventura
(Bonaventure Cemetery, Savannah)

Hay muertos sobre otros muertos allá bajo la tierra de Buenaventura,
apenas hallan sombra,
los ojos que ya nadie mira quedaron para siempre cegados por el sol
y las encinas son una procesión de fantasmas hacia el
        río Willmington,
que también es camino hacia el océano.

Basta con retroceder varios pasos,
la sangre es más espesa que el agua,
los huesos de los esclavos están cerca del río,
allí donde la tierra se confunde con el fango,
la espesa sangre,
turbia,
ciénaga donde los pies son alimento para los reptiles,
barcos de mercancía y esclavos llegan al puerto,
recogen carne y algodón para Buenaventura,
para sus árboles petrificados.

Brazos llegados de Guinea,
cinco pies de complexión negra,
muy negra,
y en la cara la marca de su país,
manglares extendiendo sus lenguas hacia el mismo océano,
temporada de lluvias sobre el río Níger
que se adentra en el continente,
en dirección contraria.

Llora una niña en medio de la pesada noche de Buenaventura,
sus lágrimas son pozos,
de ellas van a beber quienes conversan con los espíritus,

Guinea Slaves Arrive at the Plantation of Bonaventure
(Bonaventure Cemetery, Savannah)

There are dead over other dead people there under the land
      of Bonaventure,
they barely find shade,
the eyes that no one sees anymore were forever blinded by the sun
and the oaks are a procession of ghosts toward the
      Wilmington River,
which is also the way to the sea.

It suffices to go back several steps,
blood is thicker than water,
the bones of the slaves are near the river,
where the earth is mixed with mud,
thick blood,
cloudy,
a swamp where feet are food for reptiles,
merchant ships and slaves arrive at the port,
they collect meat and cotton for Bonaventure,
for its trees that have turned to stone.

Able-bodied men arrived from Guinea,
five feet, black,
very black,
and in each face the mark of their country,
mangroves spreading their tongues toward the same ocean,
rainy season on the Niger River
that flows into the continent,
in the opposite direction.

A girl cries in the middle of the heavy night of Bonaventure,
her tears are wells
those who talk to spirits will drink from,

los que habitan el borde de los resentimientos
tocados por la enfermedad,
gargantas ya rasgadas por la fiebre,
amuletos con nombre de lluvia o de montaña
se agitan para apagar la sombra,
para calmar el llanto que ahoga el sonido del río.

Tiemblan los muros de Buenaventura,
huérfanos bajo el musgo español,
las lágrimas que beben son negras como la noche oscura del verano
que trepa por los árboles.

Los caimanes no distinguen el sabor de la carne
y se deslizan bajo los humedales
para esperar.

Hay un silencio de siglos en la plantación,
un sol pesado que todo lo detiene
salvo las miradas.

Es el misterio de la tierra,
hombres que devoran hombres,
reptiles esperando una oportunidad,
barcos de mercancía que se marchan
con una carga nueva,

en dirección al sol.

those who live on the edge of resentment
touched by disease,
throats already torn by fever,
amulets with the name of rain or mountain
that they shake to put out the shadow,
to calm the crying that drowns out the sound of the river.

The walls of Bonaventure tremble,
orphans under Spanish moss,
the tears they drink are black like the dark summer night
that makes its way through the trees.

Alligators do not distinguish the taste of flesh
and they slide under the wetlands
to wait.

There is the silence of centuries on the plantation,
a heavy sun that stops everything
except the stares.

It is the mystery of earth,
men who devour men,
reptiles waiting for an opportunity,
merchant ships departing
with a new load,
                    in the direction of the sun.

El cuerpo sin vida de Hernando de Soto se hunde en el río Mississippi

Recibe en tus entrañas
a un hijo de la tierra,

traga su cuerpo,
perdona sus pecados,

lava sus sucias ropas,
arrastra su dolor

y el sufrimiento
que dejó en otros hombres.

Que el nuevo mundo lo reciba
en sus profundidades,

que el nuevo mundo le conceda
el eterno descanso.

Ya tienes en tu vientre
a un extremeño pobre

arrástralo contigo
y devuélvelo al mar

arrástralo a un viaje más largo
que cualquier ambición

sin que importe su nombre
ni su rostro.

Ya están listas
las bocas de los peces,

The Lifeless Body of Hernando de Soto Sinks in the Mississippi River

Receive in your depths
a son of the earth,

swallow his body,
forgive his sins,

wash his dirty clothes,
drag his pain

and the suffering
that he left in other men.

May the New World receive him
in its depths,

that the new world will grant
eternal rest.

You already have in your womb
a poor Extremaduran—

drag him with you
and return him to the sea

drag him on a journey longer
than any ambition

regardless of his name
or his face.

They're ready,
the mouths of the fish,

ya están listos los dientes
para cobrar el precio

de las vísceras
de quien mordió los lagos

de quien cruzó en otoño
los montes Apalaches

y atravesó la ciénaga,
y los bosques después del mar Caribe

en busca de la tierra prometida,
del Dorado en los mapas.

Ya están listos,
ya suena a funeral el viento con sus sábanas,

ya recibes la carne mordida por culebras,
la sangre devorada por la fiebre

ya es vapor en tu orilla,
reino de insectos y de barro,

masa de tiempo caminando hacia la soledad,
aquí se hunde este cuerpo miserable,

aquí se hunde la carne del primer extranjero,
del primer hombre blanco,

de un miserable hijo de la tierra
que navega en los brazos del agua más oscura.

the teeth are ready
to extract the price

for the viscera
of one who bit into the lakes

who in autumn crossed
the Appalachian Mountains

and traversed the swamps
and the forests beyond the Caribbean Sea

in search of the promised land,
El Dorado on the maps.

They are ready now,
the sheets of wind sound like a funeral,

you already receive the flesh bitten by serpents,
the blood devoured by fever,

now he is mist on your shore,
a kingdom of insects and mud,

a weight of time walking toward loneliness,
here this miserable body sinks,

here the flesh of the first foreigner sinks,
of the first white man,

of a miserable son of the earth
who sails in the arms of the darkest waters.

Butch Cassidy ingresa en la prisión estatal de Wyoming

Un nieto del imperio británico
uno de trece hermanos
el primogénito
nacido en Utah
un forajido
un atracador de bancos
un nieto de la peor cosecha
de Europa
un ganadero experto en explosivos
que conoce la ruta de los trenes
el paso de las caravanas
condenado como un vulgar ladrón de caballos
mire a la cámara
bienvenido a la prisión estatal de Wyoming
aquí no existe la vida fuera de la ley
pero tampoco las gargantas donde esconderse
bajo la tierra
espera una amnistía
una tumba sin nombre en el cementerio de San Vicente
bajo la tierra seca de Bolivia
bajo la sal y la piedra de los Andes
el nieto de un imperio
que salió a perseguir la riqueza
vientiún mil dólares del San Miguel Valley Bank de Telluride
en el polvo que asfixia
en el polvo que es lo contrario al oro
pero que es siempre el último destino
a cuatro mil quinientos metros de altitud
junto a la tumba de un minero alemán
en el pequeño cementerio de San Vicente
donde la miseria trepa sobre las lápidas
y las lenguas se borran

Butch Cassidy Enters the State Prison of Wyoming

A grandson of the British Empire
one of thirteen children
the firstborn
born in Utah
an outlaw
a bank robber
a grandchild of the worst harvest
of Europe
a ranch hand expert in explosives
who knows the schedules of the trains
the wagon trails
sentenced like a common horse thief
look at the camera
welcome to Wyoming State Penitentiary
there is no life outside the law
but neither are there gorges to hide in
underground
an amnesty awaits
an unmarked tomb in the cemetery of San Vicente
under the dry earth of Bolivia
under the salt and stone of the Andes
the grandson of an empire
who went forth in search of riches
21,000 dollars from the San Miguel Valley Bank of Telluride
in the suffocating dust
in the dust that is the opposite of gold
but that is always the final resting place
at 4,500 meters altitude
next to the grave of a German miner
in the small cemetery of San Vicente
where misery climbs the tombstones
and languages are erased

y las causas se borran
y las huellas que un día estuvieron sobre la tierra
son una herida bajo el barro
seco
tan seco como el pueblo minero de San Vicente
como un último disparo
tan sólo quiero ahorrarte el sufrimiento final
mire a la cámara
todavía no se trata de la muerte
es la prisión estatal de Wyoming
la muerte espera
no persigue
la muerte espera en una aldea de Bolivia
desata los caballos
huye
hasta volverte polvo sobre el polvo.

and the causes given up
and the tracks that once could be found on earth
are a wound under the dry mud
as dry as the mining town of San Vicente
as a last shot
I only want to save you the final suffering
look at the camera
it's still not about death
it's Wyoming State Penitentiary
death awaits
it doesn't stalk
death waits in a village in Bolivia
turn the horses loose
run for it
until returning to dust on dust.

Antonio Machado escucha las sombras del atardecer en Long Island

Te llaman Nuevo Mundo
pero cierro los ojos y el frío es una nube
que contiene la historia.

La tristeza es antigua.

Llueve,
llueve en cada palabra
y en los versos que escribo.

Estos días azules y este sol de la infancia son la lluvia
empapando una casa derruida.

La patria del dolor es el océano.

Puedo escuchar tambores victoriosos
que ensordecen la noche de los desterrados.

Puedo escuchar las nubes deslizándose,
                              las corrientes marinas
y el paso de los jóvenes trepando sobre el llanto de los embarcaderos.

Es este el porvenir,
contemplar cómo avanzan los ejércitos,
cómo el fuego devora los labios y las nubes
en un atardecer de púlpitos y sangre de inocentes,
sangre limpia y diáfana
que un día fue el amor y fue el relámpago.

Puedo escuchar, pero de nada sirve,
no sostiene mi voz el canto de los niños ni la aurora
sobre la patria ajena de la felicidad.

Antonio Machado Listens to the Shadows of the Sunset in Long Island

They call you the New World
but I close my eyes and the cold is a cloud
that envelops history.

Sorrow is ancient.

It's raining.
It rains on every word
and on the verses that I write.

These blue days and this childhood sun are the rain
soaking a house in ruins.

The ocean is the homeland of pain.

I can hear the drums of victory
that silence the night of those in exile.

I can hear the clouds floating past,
the ocean currents
and the footsteps of the young clambering over the weeping piers.

This is the future,
to contemplate how armies advance,
how fire devours lips and clouds
in a twilight of pulpits and the blood of innocents,
clean and clear blood
that once was love and lightning.

I can listen, but it's no use,
my voice does not join with the children's singing or the dawn
surrounding the foreign country of happiness.

Es este el porvenir,
una tarde de lluvia volcada en el océano,
una sombra que acecha los nombres y los cantos,
el rostro de mi madre bajo la tierra estéril.

This is the future,
an afternoon of rain spilled into the sea,
a shadow that stalks the names and songs,
the face of my mother under the barren land.

La casa de Lake Alfred

1. Ruta 66

Gordon conduce un Ford del 55 desde California hasta Florida
por una carretera que ya no existe,
bidones de agua abandonados,
moteles donde pasar la noche,
la última noche.

Gordon conduce hacia la muerte de su padre
con desesperación.

Van a ser cinco días atravesando el desierto,
cinco días sin noches, porque los faros
dejaron de funcionar,
y por eso conduce aprovechando cada minuto de sol,
como vuelan las aves migratorias,
como la última esperanza.

The House in Lake Alfred

1. Route 66

Gordon drives a '55 Ford from California to Florida
on a road that no longer exists,
abandoned water drums,
motels for spending the night,
the last night.

Gordon heads toward the death of his father
in desperation.

It will take five days to cross the desert,
five days without nights, because the headlights
stopped working,
and that's why he drives taking advantage of every minute of sun,
like migratory birds fly
like the last hope.

2. Gales–Pensilvania

Antes que casa hubo un país,
bosques y acantilados
con castillos antiguos
y lagos en los que brillan las tormentas y las auroras.

John H. Evans era un hijo de galeses pobres,
un hijo del hambre de los campesinos en los muelles del puerto
      de Liverpool,
era intensa la niebla,
apenas se avistaba la esperanza en el horizonte,
los ojos empañados tan sólo permitían mirar hacia adentro o hacia atrás.

Lo que llevaban fue todo,
porque nunca volvieron.

El hambre les persiguió hasta el fondo de la tierra,
hasta las minas de carbón de Pensilvania.

El sueño de la libertad fue un agujero en la roca
y las montañas de Gales fueron azules en sus recuerdos,
la tierra de los otros,
abandonada,
extraña,
como las vidas que un día fueron suyas pero que no pudieron llevar
      con ellos.

John H. Evans fue el primero de la familia
en nacer en America
y construyó la casa en 1923.

2. Wales–Pennsylvania

Before the house there was a country,
forests and cliffs
with ancient castles
and lakes where the storms and dawns shimmered.

John H. Evans was the son of poor Welshmen,
a child of the hunger of country folk in the docks of the port
        of Liverpool,
the fog was dense,
there was barely a glimpse of hope on the horizon,
the fogged eyes only allowed looking inward or backwards.

What they carried with them was everything,
because they would never return.

Hunger pursued them to the depths of the earth,
as far as the coal mines of Pennsylvania.

The dream of freedom was a hole in the rock
and the mountains of Wales were blue in their memories,
the land of others,
abandoned,
foreign,
like the lives that once were theirs but that they could not take
        with them.

John H. Evans was the first of the family
to be born in America
and built the house in 1923.

3. John H. Evans

Hay una lápida en el cementerio de Winter Haven con su nombre,
como si fuera posible contener
en las palabras escritas sobre la piedra
su trabajo en los huertos, los campos de naranjas
y los versos de Kipling que aprendió de memoria
y que recitaba marcando el ritmo
sobre la mesa, en el porche.

John H. Evans no murió en la casa que construyó para su familia,
los médicos explicaron que sus arterias se habían endurecido
y poco a poco su memoria se fue borrando de la tierra,
y allí se fue perdiendo,
desorientado,
cada día más solo en el cuerpo de otro hombre
irreconocible.
No alcanzó a despedirse de nadie,
tampoco de su mujer que había abandonado el mundo hacía seis años
y cuya ausencia pudo sentir como un vacío
sin nombre, ni rostro.

3. John H. Evans

There is a gravestone in the Winter Haven cemetery with his name,
as if it were possible to contain
in words written on the stone
his work in the groves, the fields of oranges
and the verses of Kipling that he learned by heart
and that he recited while keeping time
on the table, on the porch.

John H. Evans did not die in the house he built for his family,
the doctors explained that his arteries had hardened
and little by little his memory was erased from the earth,
and there he was losing himself,
disoriented,
each day more alone in the body of another
unrecognizable man.
He did not manage to say goodbye to anyone,
not even his wife who had left the world six years before
and whose absence felt like an emptiness
without name or face.

4. Artemisa

La abuela Artemisa no quería morirse,
le daba pena,
no era cuestión de miedo ni de falta de fe,
su gravedad era otra:
amaba demasiadas cosas en el mundo,
sencillamente,
amaba su huerto de rosas al otro lado de la casa,
y cocinar trigo bueno,
y el olor de la infancia en la tierra de México
antes de que cinco mil hombres armados arrasaran la hacienda.

Artemisa estaba llena de secretos que nunca contó a nadie
porque tampoco nadie preguntaba.

Una tarde presintió su final y desde entonces
se fue borrando del mundo
resistiéndose
pensando en arrancar el cáncer de su cuerpo
con un cuchillo o con las uñas
porque la vida era demasiado hermosa.

Su corazón se detuvo en un atardecer rosado
mientras todas las aves gritaban espantadas.

4. Artemisa

Grandma Artemisa did not want to die,
it upset her,
it was not a matter of fear or lack of faith,
her concern was different:
she loved the things of the world too much,
simply,
she loved her rose garden on the other side of the house,
and to cook trigo bueno,
and the smell of childhood in the land of Mexico
before 5,000 armed men razed the hacienda.

Artemisa was full of secrets that she never told anyone
but neither did anyone ask.

One afternoon she sensed her end and since then
she slowly took leave of the world
resisting
planning to pluck cancer from her body
with a knife or her fingernails
because life was too beautiful.

Her heart stopped on an evening the color of roses
while all the birds cried out in fright.

5. Arthur McNeer y Florence Root

Gordon piensa que el desierto es inmenso,
arena sobre arena,
del mismo modo que sucede con la nieve
que cae sobre otra nieve
sobre las lejanas tierras de Alaska
a las que su abuelo Arthur llegó en busca de oro
con Florence, que nunca quiso perseguir la riqueza,
pero que subió a un barco en el puerto de Seattle
hacia un lugar desconocido.

Juntos atravesaron bosques y desiertos sembrados
de ilusiones
brillantes
tan brillantes
que relucían dentro de la tierra.

Arthur y Florence
compraron una parcela con una veta de oro en su corazón
y enterraron junto a un río la esperanza escrita en un papel,
el título de propiedad,
la tinta sobre la que se edifica el porvenir.

Querían poner a salvo el futuro bajo la tierra
y cuando regresaron
bajo la tierra: nada,
allí no estaba el futuro, ni el pasado,
ni el recuerdo del pasado,
todo se esfumó del mismo modo
que un sueño
                en los brazos del amanecer
de los bandidos
o de la mala suerte.

5. Arthur McNeer and Florence Root

Gordon thinks the desert is immense,
sand on sand,
in the same way that happens with snow
that falls on other snow
across the distant lands of Alaska
to which his grandfather Arthur arrived to look for gold
with Florence, who never wanted to pursue riches,
but they boarded a ship in the port of Seattle
to an unknown place.

Together they crossed forests and deserts sown
with bright hopes
so bright
that they shone within the earth.

Arthur and Florence
bought a plot with a vein of gold in its heart
and buried their hopes beside a river, written on a piece of paper,
the deed to the property,
the ink on which the future is built.

They meant to save their future under the earth
and when they returned
under the earth: nothing,
there was no future and no past,
nor the memory of the past,
everything vanished like
a dream
          in the arms of the dawn
of bandits
or bad luck.

6. Base aérea de Edwards, California

Gordon intenta conducir de noche,
treinta y cinco millas por hora por la ruta 40 son suficientes para
      salirse de la carretera
y obligarle a parar.

Frente a la entrada de la base aérea permanece el único recuerdo
      del viaje
atravesando America
de oeste a este,
en dirección contraria al sol
y a los barcos que zarpan desde Liverpool.

Todo lo demás es el miedo,
la carretera que conduce al miedo,
lo inevitable,
la agonía que se arrastra como un reptil.

6. Edwards Air Force Base, California

Gordon tries to drive at night,
thirty-five miles per hour on Interstate 40 is enough to get off
      the highway
and force him to stop.

The entrance of the air force base remains the only memory of
      his trip
crossing America
from west to east,
in the opposite direction to the sun
and to the ships that sail from Liverpool.

Everything else is fear,
the road that leads to fear,
that which is inevitable,
the agony that drags itself along like a reptile.

7. Artemisa María Consuelo Ramonet

Es el día del cumpleaños de su madre,
pero su madre ha muerto
hace más de diez años.

La encuentra junto al comedor
y no va a decirle nada,
puede estar en su casa,
todo sigue
como lo dejó,
los libros, los cuadros,
los platos de porcelana y las mecedoras,
también la ropa en los armarios,
incluso los manteles.

Ahora que los dos son huérfanos
no van a dirigirse palabra alguna.

Gordon observa la camisa blanca
y el vestido azul de su madre
que no deja de mirar al suelo,
como quien sueña de una manera triste.

Tal vez ella conoce cómo acaban los sueños,
tal vez por eso calla.

7. Artemisa María Consuelo Ramonet

It's his mother's birthday,
but his mother has been dead
more than ten years.

He finds her next to the dining room
and she will not tell him anything.
He can be at home in her house,
everything goes on
as she left it,
the books, the paintings,
porcelain plates and rocking chairs,
also the clothes in the closets,
even the tablecloths.

Now that the two of them are orphans
they are not going to speak a single word to each other.

Gordon looks at the white blouse
and the blue skirt worn by his mother
who does not stop looking down at the floor,
like someone who dreams sadly.

Maybe she knows how dreams end,
maybe that's why she is silent.

8. Lake Alfred, Florida

Sólo unas millas separan a Gordon de la casa de Lake Alfred,
le atormenta la idea de no encontrar a su padre con vida,
pero también
asomarse a los ojos de su desolación.

El final de la carretera
será las más oscuras lágrimas,
el llanto de su padre por la vida,
y un agujero en la tierra
que aguarda
vacío
la inminente noticia de la muerte.

8. Lake Alfred, Florida

Only a few miles separate Gordon from the house in Lake Alfred,
he is tormented by the idea of not finding his father alive,
but also by the idea
of seeing the despair in his eyes.

The end of the road
will bring the darkest tears,
the cry of his father for life,
and a hole in the earth
that awaits
empty
the imminent news of death.

La balada de Nueva Inglaterra

Love is anterior to life

Emily Dickinson

Two roads diverged in a yellow wood

Robert Frost

Después del mar, de todo el mar, la tierra fría,
el viento helado que llega desde Nueva Escocia
y es un cangrejo de nieve en las botas de un pescador de Maine
que regresa a casa para la cena,
una sopa caliente le devuelve el color rosado de los labios,
después observa arder un tronco en la chimenea,
sólo el fuego ha aprendido a trepar sobre el frío,
no es demasiado feroz para quien ha visto el mar
        levantando una tormenta.

Las orillas del norte son un lamento,
el llanto desciende por sus desfiladeros
hasta tocar la superficie del oleaje,
en las rocas
queda su marca, como en los rostros
de quienes han sufrido
deja el dolor su ruina.

En los puertos del norte amanece temprano
y la vida es tan vieja como un lobo de mar.

Esta es la orilla de los primeros colonos
procedentes de la isla más antigua del mundo,
llegaron persiguiendo las oportunidades,
siguiendo las corrientes marinas
mientras rezaban,

The Balada of New England

Love is anterior to life

Emily Dickinson

Two roads diverged in a yellow wood

Robert Frost

After the sea, the whole sea, the cold land,
the icy wind that comes from Nova Scotia
and is a snow crab in the boots of a Maine fisherman
who comes home for dinner,
a bowl of hot soup returns the rosiness to his lips,
then he watches a log burn in the fireplace,
only fire has learned to climb on the cold,
it's not that fierce for someone who has seen the sea
      rising in a storm.

The northern shores are a lament,
the crying descends through gorges
until it touches the surface of the waves,
on the rocks
its mark remains, as in the faces
of those who have suffered,
pain leaves its ruin.

In the northern ports dawn comes early
and life is as ancient as an old sea lion.

This is the shore of the first colonists
from the oldest island in the world,
they came chasing opportunities,
following the ocean currents
while they prayed,

llegaron porque siguieron la palabra de Dios
hasta una orilla de piedras tocadas por el llanto
sobre el mismo océano del que partieron.

Trajeron las canciones,
las redes,
las palabras,
trajeron el anzuelo y las iglesias,
pero también el pecado.

El diablo persigue sus oportunidades.

Cuelgan los cuerpos de las brujas en Nueva Inglaterra,
cuelgan frente a la muchedumbre
a unos pasos del puerto de Salem
donde se embarcan cada noche los pescadores
en dirección a la tierra que fue origen.

En los puertos del norte la vida es un regreso
con olor a pescado.

Es la hora de Nueva Inglaterra,
el sol
avanza como un viejo puritano
y se levanta sobre el océano
y da partida al vuelo de los pájaros,
que alumbran una ventana de Amherst
donde los ojos de una mujer contemplan el mundo,
el amor es anterior a la vida,
pero se alza con los pájaros del amanecer frente a su ventana.

Avanza el sol sobre las huellas de los hombres,
avanza sobre los árboles, se refleja en los lagos,
sigue su ruta de manera estricta,
                              sin desviarse,

they came because they followed the word of God
to a rocky shore touched by tears shed
over the same ocean from whence they came.

They brought the songs,
the nets,
their words,
they brought the hook and their churches,
but also sin.

The devil pursues his own opportunities.

The bodies of the witches of New England are hanging,
they hang before the multitude
a few steps from Salem Harbor
where fishermen set out each night
in the direction of the land of their birth.

In the northern ports, life comes back
with the smell of fish.

It's New England time,
the sun
comes like an old Puritan
and it rises over the ocean
and gives leave to the flight of the birds,
it lights a window in Amherst
where the eyes of a woman contemplate the world,
love is anterior to life,
but it departs with the birds of the dawn through her window.

The sun comes on the footprints of men,
it comes over the trees, it is reflected in the lakes,
it follows its route strictly,
                              without going off course,

con una voluntad que sólo da la fe,
la fe
que llegó con los primeros barcos
para poblar montañas.

Pero con ella también llegó la indecisión
y la duda,
el este
y el oeste,
los ojos vigilantes,
las razas,
los anzuelos,
los domingos, hasta los continentes
sin líneas en los mapas,
pero también los mapas
con sus bordes,
la libertad,
los dos caminos que se bifurcan en un bosque amarillo.

Ha llegado la hora de Nueva Inglaterra,
el sol avanza desde el este como un barco empujado por el porvenir.

with a will that only faith can provide,
the faith
that arrived with the first ships
to populate mountains.

But with it also came indecision
and doubt,
the East
and the West,
watchful eyes,
races,
hooks,
Sundays, even continents
without lines on the maps,
but also the maps
with their borders,
freedom,
the roads that diverge in a yellow wood.

New England's time has come,
the sun comes from the east like a ship sent forth by the future.

LA PATRIA ES UNA MADRE QUE
REPARTE LA SUERTE ENTRE
LAS BOCAS

THE COUNTRY IS A MOTHER
WHO DISTRIBUTES LUCK AMONG
THE MOUTHS

Abandoné al país donde me alimentaron.
Con los que me olvidaron se poblaría una ciudad.

Quit the country that bore and nursed me.
Those who forgot me would make a city.

Joseph Brodsky, "May 24, 1980"

Raza

Porque todos los padres y las madres de mis padres,
todo el tiempo pasado,

                son tierra.

Pero también idioma,
palabras como *español, gitano, negro* o *inmigrante.*
Palabras que se levantan como espadas, muros que son construidos
       con palabras,
los viejos continentes, los nuevos continentes,
with the fading kingdoms and kings over there,
sobre las mismas ruinas,
sobre los mitos y los oráculos,

                se levanta America.

En ella se derraman los hijos de los hijos de los nietos de
       las civilizaciones.
Hijos de Roma y Grecia, pobladores de Egipto, nómadas de la India,
sus ríos desembocan en el vientre del Mississippi,
traen el agua en sus venas, riegan la tierra fértil
y después son alimento para los árboles,
oxígeno en los pulmones de otros hombres,
agua otra vez en combinación con el hidrógeno.

America se riega con la sangre de las civilizaciones.

Pasado es la palabra que guarda el equilibrio sobre sus labios,
el presente es ayer,
el futuro es ayer,
el fruto después de una tormenta fue mordido.

Digo *español,* y no entiendo.
Digo *España,* y se llenan mis ojos de melancolía

Race

Because all the fathers and mothers of my parents,
all time past,

       are earth.

But also language,
words like *Spanish, gypsy, black,* or *immigrant.*
Words that rise like swords, walls that are constructed
  with words,
the old continents, the new continents,
with the fading kingdoms and kings over there,
on the same ruins,
on the myths and oracles,

        America rises.

Into her pour the children of the children of the grandchildren
  of civilizations.
Children of Rome and Greece, settlers of Egypt, nomads of India,
their rivers flow into the womb of the Mississippi,
they bring the water in their veins, they water the fertile land
and then they are food for the trees,
oxygen in the lungs of other men,
water again in combination with hydrogen.

America is watered with the blood of civilizations.

Past is the word that keeps the balance on their lips,
the present is yesterday,
the future is yesterday,
the fruit after a storm was bitten.

I say *Spanish,* and I do not understand.
I say *Spain,* and my eyes fill with melancholy

pero también mi pecho de flores apagadas, de un sabor mineral,
como si fuera el humo de un incendio lejano.

Sólo el color de la tierra donde crecí es tan cierto
                                    como una raza.
Una tierra rojiza, muchas veces bañada por la sangre.
Tierra que vio morir a fenicios, romanos,
árabes, hombres
de toda tierra y patria,
y también a mi abuelo,
y al padre de mi abuelo,
y a las viejas beatas que acuden cada mañana a la parroquia de San
        Juan de Dios,
y a los hombres que tratan de cruzar el estrecho y son devueltos a la
        orilla de mi país
por las olas del Mediterráneo,
y a las gentes que sufren y miran siempre a la tierra por vergüenza o
        por debilidad,
o simplemente porque quieren terminar el viaje.

Mi raza es esa tierra,
y la palabra *tierra*,
y el agua que la limpia
sin prestar atención
a
la
sangre
que
arrastra.

but also my heart with flowers gone, of a mineral taste,
as if it were the smoke of a distant fire.

Only the color of the land where I grew up is as certain
                                as a race.
A reddish earth, often bathed in blood.
Land that saw Phoenicians die, Romans,
Arabs, men
of every land and country,
and also my grandfather,
and my grandfather's father,
and also the old nuns who come every morning to the parish of
       San Juan de Dios,
and the men who try to cross the strait and are returned to the shores
       of my country
by the waves of the Mediterranean,
and the people who suffer and always look toward the ground out of
       shame or weakness,
or simply because they want to put an end to the journey.

My race belongs to that land,
the word *land,*
and the water that cleans it
without paying heed
to
the
blood
that
drags it away.

La patria es una madre que reparte la suerte entre las bocas

Haber nacido
con esta lengua de palabras
y de ceniza.
Haber visto a la luz abrirse paso
en un país
fusiles apuntando al enemigo,
en un país
madre de todos mis iguales,
todos abriendo la boca al mismo tiempo,
el hambre señalando con desigual fortuna,
eso es la patria.

Santificado sea su nombre,
su marca en el esmalte
y en la cara mordida por la viruela,
sus hijos
ven las altas mareas,
divisan barcos,
los sueños detenidos
ondulan como guerra,
ahora ya pueden
sacrificar sus vidas,
ahora ya están listos,
han navegado
por la tempestad,
han dejado los sueños
flotando
igual que mercancía
que un día fue alimento,
han sentido la duda
y han gritado,
insatisfechos,

The Country Is a Mother Who Distributes Luck among the Mouths

To have been born
with this language of words
and of ashes.
To have seen the light breaking through
in a country
with rifles trained on the enemy,
in a country
mother of all my equals,
all opening their mouths at the same time,
hunger choosing with unequal fortunes,
that is the homeland.

Blessed be its name,
its mark etched on the teeth
and in the face bitten by smallpox,
its children
see the high seas,
they sight ships,
their interrupted dreams
rippling like war,
now they can
sacrifice their lives,
now they are ready,
they have braved
storms,
they have left their dreams
floating
like cargo
that once nourished them,
they have felt doubt
and they have cried out,
dissatisfied,

hambrientos y traidores,
fusiles apuntando
al enemigo,
en un país,
hecho de tierra y sangre.

hungry and betrayed,
rifles trained
on the enemy,
in a country,
made of earth and blood.

La ceguera

Si la ceguera es

                      negra

cuál será el color de la muerte.

Negra como la piel de un hombre

                    negro,

la ceguera,

también es   blanca

cuando arranca los párpados

cuando invade la voz y las palabras

ciegas

como la luz que deslumbra,

como los hombres que escrutan en la piel

el brillo.

Es sábado,

el día del milagro,

alguien escupe a la tierra,

su saliva y el polvo son el barro en los ojos del mendigo,

que va a lavarse para ver

                    el pecado

que deslumbra,   blanco,

como la sangre,

de qué color será el mundo

cuando ya no estemos,

de qué color es la palabra *siempre,*

o la palabra   *mundo,*

o la palabra   *negro.*

The Blindness

If blindness is

                      black

what will be the color of death.

Black as a man's skin

                      black,

the blindness,
is also   white
when it tears away the eyelids
when it invades the voice and the words
blind
like the light that dazzles,
like men scrutinizing the sheen
on the skin.

It's Saturday,
the day of the miracle,
someone spits on the ground,
his saliva and dust are mud in the eyes of the beggar,
who is going to wash to see

                      sin

that dazzles,   white,
like blood,
what color will the world be
when we are no longer,
what color is the word *always*,
or the word   *world,*
or the word   *black.*

La soledad es un invierno frente al mar del pasado

La playa es solitaria,
hay un vacío en los años,
era ayer,
yo estaba allí tendido,
llegaron unas voces familiares,
me despertaron
pero ya nadie había,
entonces quise
caminar tras las huellas,
perseguir esas voces
que no sonaban ya
pero que estaban
latiendo
dentro de mis oídos,
dentro de mi inquietud
y caminé,
caminé sin apenas detenerme
hasta verme a mí mismo
en medio de una playa solitaria,
vacía,
justo antes
de adentrarme en el mar
persiguiendo unas voces,
justo antes,
de la ausencia,
del mar,
de ti.

Solitude Is a Winter before the Sea of the Past

The beach is lonely,
there is a gap between the years,
it was yesterday,
I was lying there,
there came familiar voices
that woke me up,
but nobody was there anymore,
then I wanted
to walk in their footsteps,
pursue those voices
that did not make a sound
but which were
sounding
inside my ears,
within my concern
and I walked,
I walked hardly stopping
until I saw myself
in the middle of a lonely beach,
empty,
just before
getting into the sea
chasing some voices,
just before,
absence,
from the sea,
of you.

Ruby Bridges camina con escolta federal hacia la tierra prometida

Cada mañana Ruby atraviesa el desierto
persigue la promesa de que al final del camino
manará leche y miel
pero la gente escupe
                        la multitud escupe
y cuando siente sed el agua está salada.

Ruby camina cada amanecer con el almuerzo en una pequeña bolsa
porque el final del camino es dulce
porque el final del camino está lleno de frutos
envenenados
para su boca sobre la que escupe la multitud
que defiende la tierra bañada por el Mississippi
cultivada por los esclavos
cuanto más oprimidos más
se multiplicaban
los negros del río Mississippi
si es niño debe morir
si es niña se le permite la vida
pero no la tierra
sobre la que Ruby Bridges camina cada mañana
con determinación
sobre la que también avanzan las madres cargando un ataúd y una
        muñeca negra
para Ruby
para su voluntad
porque quienes se mantengan firmes
verán el agua amarga convertida en dulce
porque ellos fueron elegidos por su insignificancia
verán desalojadas a las más grandes naciones.

Ruby Bridges Walks with Federal Escort to the Promised Land

Every morning Ruby crosses the desert
pursues the promise that at the end of the road
milk and honey will flow
but people are spitting
                     the crowd is spitting
and when she feels thirsty the water tastes of salt.

Ruby walks each dawn with lunch in a small bag
because the end of the road is sweet
because the end of the road is full of fruits
poisoned
for her mouth, spat upon by the crowd
that defends the land bathed by the Mississippi
worked by slaves
the more oppressed the more
they multiplied
the Black people of the Mississippi River
if it's a boy he must die
if it's a girl, she's allowed to live
but not the land
on which Ruby Bridges walks every morning
determined
that the mothers also move forward, carrying a coffin with a
       black doll
for Ruby
for her courage
because those who stand firm
will see the bitter water turn sweet
because they were chosen for their insignificance
they will see the greatest of nations thrown out.

JFK abandona la patria para conquistar la muerte

Se acerca   el corazón   de America.

Escuchen cómo gritan en las calles,
cómo celebran su nombre,
su palabra,
su juventud ...

El futuro no puede estar en manos de la juventud,
el futuro es de la patria
pero ellos gritan desde las aceras de Main Street
todos quieren verlo pasar
todos quieren estar cerca de la esperanza
como si fuera posible tocarla con los dedos
o alcanzarla con la mirada
o con un disparo definitivo.

La patria es una ventana en el sexto piso de un almacén de libros,
es un rifle en las manos de Lee Harvey Oswald,
es un aparcamiento al otro lado de la carretera tras una colina
        de hierba.

Silencio

Es imposible el silencio porque todos gritan
y sus voces se alzan como una ciudad dorada sobre una montaña
porque han dejado de preguntarse
qué puede hacer por ellos su país
y ahora están dispuestos a conquistarlo.

Ya se acerca
                    el corazón   de America,
todos pueden sentir sus latidos desde cualquier parte
porque son los latidos de todos.

JFK Leaves the Country to Conquer Death

The heart   of America   comes close.

Listen to how they cry out in the streets,
how they celebrate his name,
his words,
his youth . . .

The future cannot rest in the hands of youth,
the future belongs to the country
but they shout from the sidewalks of Main Street
all want to see him pass by
all want to be close to his hope
as if it were possible to touch it with their fingers
or reach it with a glance
or with a last shot.

The country is a window on the sixth floor of a book depository,
it's a rifle in the hands of Lee Harvey Oswald,
it is a parking lot on the other side of the road behind a grassy knoll.

Silence

Silence is impossible because everyone is shouting
and their voices rise like a golden city on the hill
because they have stopped wondering
what their country can do for them
and now are willing to conquer it.

It's drawing close now
the heart   of America,
everyone can feel their heartbeats everywhere
because they are the heartbeats of everyone.

Pero la patria no tiene corazón,
nadie la ha visto nunca consolando a un extraño
o llorando a un hijo muerto, desesperada.

La patria tiene el pulso
frío
desde una ventana
frío
desde una colina
alguien abre un paraguas negro bajo el sol en Dealey Plaza
el corazón de America está en Houston con Elm Street
y avanza lentamente hacia su destino
mientras la gente grita.

Silencio

Silencio

Silencio

La patria ya está a salvo,
ya pueden encender sus televisores,
ya están listos los comunicados.

La patria es una equis sobre la carretera
en el mismo lugar que la esperanza.

Sólo quien conquista el miedo puede conquistar la muerte.

But the country has no heart,
no one has ever seen her comforting a stranger
or weeping over a dead son, desperately.

The country has a cold
pulse
from a window
cold
from a hill
someone opens a black umbrella under the sun in Dealey Plaza
the heart of America is in Houston with Elm Street
and moves slowly toward its destination
while people shout.

Silence

Silence

Silence

The country is safe now,
You can now turn on your TVs,
communications are ready.

The country is an X on the road
in the place where hope was.

Only those who conquer fear can conquer death.

SHOOTINGS

Happiness is a warm gun.

John Lennon

¡El diablo ha enloquecido!

The devil has gone mad!

Attila József

Austin, Texas, 1966.

No seré yo quien dispare
será otro hombre
o diablo
quien apunte
desde la torre
porque pienso en subir a la torre cada día
he intentado escapar de mis propios pensamientos
pero hay algo dentro de mi cabeza
una semilla
o un escorpión
o una bala
con mi nombre
Charles
quisiera abrirme el cráneo con un cincel para poder sacarlo
Charles Whitman
el elegido para subir a lo alto de la torre
y repartir lo que me ha sido entregado
                                    en abundancia
y sembrarlo con la precisión de un ejército
porque soy un soldado
                    el marine Charles Whitman
alguna vez fue manchada mi reputación
pero desde la torre el pasado queda en un lugar casi irreconocible
lejano
pequeño
insignificante
sólo importa el ahora
sobre el reloj
no hay tiempo para mirar atrás
todos van a pensar en el futuro
todos van a correr hacia donde puedan encontrar compasión
        o arrepentimiento

Austin, Texas, 1966.

I will not be the one to shoot
it will be another man
or a devil
who takes aim
from the tower
because I think about going up into the tower every day
I have tried to escape from my thoughts
but there is something inside my head
a seed
or a scorpion
or a bullet
with my name
Charles
I would like to open my skull with a chisel to take it out
Charles Whitman
the one chosen to climb to the top of the tower
and distribute what has been given to me
                                    in abundance
and sow it with military precision
because I am a soldier
                    the marine Charles Whitman
at times my reputation was tainted
but from the tower the past is almost unrecognizable
it is far
and small
insignificant
only this moment matters
on the clock
there is no time to look back
everyone will be thinking about the future
everyone will run toward compassion
or repentance

y yo no puedo dárselas

mis virtudes son otras

de las que todos huyen

mientras mis pensamientos los persiguen

con mira telescópica

no puedo hacer ya nada por evitarlo

he matado a mi madre

y a mi mujer

no puedo hacer ya nada para evitar la muerte porque todo lo ocupa

soy un esclavo

nadie vaya a culparme

no manchen la reputación del soldado Charles Whitman

soy un inocente

tal vez alguna vez fui irrespetuoso

pero fui entrenado para la obediencia

no me atrevería a cuestionar ninguna orden

he arrancado un ramillete de flores

siento dentro un relámpago

son las pisadas de los animales

bolas de fuego

el campo de batalla

y estas agujas

mi madre agonizando

yo también me quedaré mudo cuando se acabe la munición

pero no pienso arrodillarme

he sido hecho prisionero

sé lo que significa estar encerrado

en una celda

o un cráneo

una ráfaga más

la humedad en Florida será insoportable

qué mala época para un entierro

Charles Whitman

una bandera cubrirá mi ataúd

and I cannot give it to them
my virtues are other
than those from which they all flee
while my thoughts follow them
with my telescopic sight
I cannot do anything now to avoid it
I have killed my mother
and my wife
I cannot do anything now to avoid death because it is everywhere
I am its slave
nobody is going to blame me
do not tarnish the reputation of soldier Charles Whitman
I am an innocent
maybe I was once disrespectful
but I was trained to be obedient
I would not dare to question any order
I have plucked a bouquet of flowers
I feel a lightning flash inside
and the trampling of animals
balls of fire
the battlefield
and these needles
my mother dying
I too will be quiet when the ammunition runs out
but I do not plan on kneeling
I have been taken prisoner
I know what it means to be locked
in a cell
or a skull
one more burst
the humidity in Florida will be unbearable
what a bad time for a funeral

                        Charles Whitman

a flag will cover my coffin

qué desgraciado
he estado demasiado tiempo en los brazos de las tinieblas
ya es hora de ascender majestuosamente
una vez esté fuera de mi cuerpo todos quedaremos aliviados
pero no vayan a culparme
no maldigan el nombre de Charles Whitman
porque todo estaba dispuesto
en el reloj
en el cráneo
en el rifle
en la torre
en el infierno

what a wretch
I have been too long in the arms of darkness
it's time to ascend majestically
once I am out of my body we will all be relieved
but they should not blame me
they should not curse the name of Charles Whitman
because everything was set
on the clock
in the skull
in the rifle
in the tower
in hell

Columbine High School, Littleton, Colorado, 1999.

Permíteme mostrarte lo que pienso de ti.

Puedes mirar las marcas de mis muñecas,
me he golpeado a mí mismo
muchas
noches
para poder dormir,
recibe todo esto a cambio de tu odio,
dulces sueños,
voy a morderte,
ya no me queda tiempo para elegir,
los más bellos primero,
hoy es el último día,
es el aniversario,
dime algo hermoso,
he venido a derramar mis semillas,
voy a pisarte camino de   la inmortalidad:

date la vuelta

                              aléjate
ya todo ha sido dicho

el mañana

                              es una bandera

el mañana

                              es una bala entre la espina
                              dorsal y la aorta

el mañana

                              es un lugar vacío

Columbine High School, Littleton, Colorado, 1999.

Let me show you what I think of you.

You can look at the scars on my wrists,
I have cut myself
many
nights
in order to sleep,
receive all this in exchange for your hatred,
sweet dreams,
I'm gonna bite you,
I don't have time to choose
so the most beautiful first.
Today is our last day,
it's the anniversary,
tell me something beautiful,
I have come to spill my seed,
I'm gonna step on you on my way   to immortality:

turn around

                              get away
everything has already been said

tomorrow

                              is a flag

tomorrow

                              is a bullet between the spine
                              and the aorta

tomorrow

                              is an empty place

el mañana

                es un error de cálculo

el mañana

                es un sueño demasiado
                dulce

¿No tienes la impresión de que el mundo

                es extraordinariamente
                pequeño?

Recuerda todo esto cuando te creas
libre.

tomorrow

                            is a miscalculation

tomorrow

                            is a dream too sweet

Don't you have the impression that the world

                            is extraordinarily small?

Remember all this when you believe
you are free.

Virginia Tech, Blacksburg, Virginia, 2007.

La soledad es el silencio más profundo,
las palabras son balas en dirección a uno mismo,
no saciaría vuestra curiosidad
con palabras,
porque me muerden las conversaciones
que suceden a mi alrededor,
no saciaría
la indiferencia con palabras,
de nada serviría
explicar el silencio inexplicable.

Pero ahogar las gargantas
no es cuestión de saciar,
es cuestión de llevar el silencio a todas las bocas
que son ruido a mi paso,
un murmullo,
el público mortal.

Si os encuentro
podría saludaros,
174 balas,
obedeciendo las indicaciones del fabricante,
arma semiautomática,
deberían mostrar respeto ante los cañones
porque van a liberarnos de todo sufrimiento,
si son agradecidos
dejarán de arrastrarse,
son 174 disparos,
el último en la sien,
la sudorosa sien
que conduce al final de todos los murmullos.

Virginia Tech, Blacksburg, Virginia, 2007.

Solitude is the deepest silence,
the words are bullets in the direction of oneself,
I would not satisfy your curiosity
with words,
because I'm wounded by conversations
that happen around me,
I would not sate
indifference with words,
nothing would do
to explain the inexplicable silence.

It's not a matter of satisfying,
it's a matter of bringing silence to all mouths
that are noise in my path,
a whispering,
the deadly public.

If I find you
maybe I'll say hello,
174 bullets
obeying the manufacturer's instructions,
a semiautomatic weapon,
they should show respect facing the barrels
because the bullets are going to free us from all suffering,
if they were grateful
they would stop dragging themselves,
there are 174 shots,
the last one in the temple,
the sweaty temple
that leads to the end of all the whispers.

Westroads Mall, Omaha, Nebraska, 2007.

Alguien tiene que recolectar
la siembra,
el fruto de la bestia y sus semillas
esparcidas por todo el condado
en las oficinas
en los parques
en los hospitales
psiquiátricos
he robado 17 dólares
en una cadena de hamburguesas
en las gasolineras
el odio
puede medirse en galones
llévame
de la mano
no hay que temer
la cosecha
en las estanterías
hay flores enterradas
yo solamente soy el elegido
el diablo es un rifle semiautomático
el diablo es un AK-47 de fabricación soviética con
        múltiples modernizaciones
ya nadie puede salvarme
de la fama
de la abundancia
tengo sangre en los dientes
que todo el mundo cierre
los ojos
el diablo es un AK-74 de fabricación rusa
la felicidad es esta esclavitud
no finjan que son inocentes

Westroads Mall, Omaha, Nebraska, 2007.

Someone has to gather
what has been sown,
the fruit of the beast and its seeds
scattered throughout the county
in the offices
in the parks
in psychiatric hospitals
I stole seventeen dollars
from a hamburger place
at the gas station
hatred
can be measured in gallons
take me
by the hand
there is no need to fear
the harvest
on the bookshelves
there are buried flowers
I'm just the chosen one
the devil is a semiautomatic rifle
the devil is a Soviet-made AK-47 with upgrades
no one can save me anymore
from the fame
of abundance
I have tasted blood
everyone should close
their eyes
the devil is a Russian-made AK-74
happiness is this bondage
do not pretend that you are innocent

alguien
tendrá la ocasión de disfrutar
no voy a renunciar a ella
el diablo es un Kalashnikov,
un WASR-10 en su versión nacional,
fabricado en St. Albans, Vermont,
esto que ven tan sólo son unos brazos
no vayan a juzgarme
no adelanten los acontecimientos
cuando apaguen las luces
vamos a reírnos juntos en la oscuridad.

someone

will have the chance to enjoy

I will not give up on this

the devil is a Kalashnikov,

a WASR-10 in its country of origin,

manufactured in St. Albans, Vermont,

what you are seeing is only a few of the arms

do not go judging me

do not rush things

when they turn off the lights

we will have a good laugh together in the dark.

Sandy Hook Elementary School, Newtown, Connecticut, 2012.

Si he matado a mi madre,
puedo matar a todos los hijos de la tierra.

Llega el dolor por todas rendijas,
viaja en las tuberías,
haré sonar con rabia los tambores,
ya pueden comenzar a preparar los funerales,
los valientes soldados vestirán con sus trajes relucientes,
he matado a mi madre,
no será muy difícil disparar al corazón de la patria,
a su opulencia,
mi alma está podrida como lo están los muertos,
siento el hedor,
es como un manantial
que recorre el país de norte a sur.

Sandy Hook Elementary School, Newtown, Connecticut, 2012.

If I killed my mother,
I can kill all the children of the earth.

The pain comes through all the openings,
it travels through the pipes,
I will bang the drums with rage,
you can start preparing the funerals,
the brave soldiers will wear their dress uniforms,
I have killed my mother,
it will not be difficult to shoot at the heart of the country,
at its opulence,
my soul is rotten like the dead,
I smell the stench,
it's like a spring
that travels the country from north to south.

Pulse, Orlando, Florida, 2016.

Aunque el amor no deje de ser dulce hecho al amanecer.

Jaime Gil de Biedma

Los amantes no tienen vocación de morir.

Vicente Aleixandre

Apenas una boca,
unos labios,
la lengua,
otros no fueron más que el viento,
ojos hundidos sobre la multitud,
alguien dijo: "Hace frío",
apenas diez segundos antes de las primeras ráfagas.

Llega la hora de los amantes
como si fuera el alba,
llega la hora con un fusil de asalto,
es el amanecer
que ya conoce el día al otro lado,
nadie enciende la luz para mirar el rostro de los hombres,
los amantes no tienen vocación de morir,
y se resisten, gritan, se retuercen
y ven brotar la sangre
que es el agua más fría
que es la playa más solitaria del pasado.

El silencio final fue tan ruidoso
que nadie quiso abrir los ojos ni la boca.

Pulse, Orlando, Florida, 2016.

Although love does not stop being sweet done at sunrise.

Jaime Gil de Biedma

Lovers do not have a vocation to die.

Vicente Aleixandre

Just a mouth,
a pair of lips,
a tongue,
others were no more than the wind,
eyes settling on the crowd,
someone said: "It's cold,"
barely ten seconds before the first shots.

The time for lovers has come
as if it were the dawn,
the time comes for an assault rifle,
it is dawn
and already knows the day on the other side,
no one turns on the lights to look at the faces of men,
lovers do not have a vocation to die,
and they resist, they scream, they writhe
and they see the blood spurt
that is the coldest water
that is the loneliest beach of the past.

The final silence was so loud
that no one wanted to open their eyes or their mouths.

Mandalay Bay Hotel, Las Vegas, Nevada, 2017.

Un lobo solitario,
    en sus ojos el humo.
Un solo tirador,
    en sus ojos la muerte
       con sus dados,
el azar
el azar
el azar   es un arma automática
un lobo del desierto
    que observa la multitud
desde el piso 32 del hotel Mandalay Bay,
las cámaras de seguridad muestran
su determinación,
    Nevada,
en sus ojos la arena brilla como el cristal
     roto
silba el aire y ayuda a respirar se llenan
    los pulmones.

Un hombre acostumbrado a ver girar la suerte
va a sujetar ahora la suerte de los otros,
sólo vive del juego quien confía en la llama,
quien persigue la llama aunque le queme,
     por mucho que le queme,
las cámaras de seguridad muestran
la firmeza del pulso,
    el paso lento
     y constante
      de la muerte.

Stephen Paddock,
64 años,

Mandalay Bay Hotel, Las Vegas, Nevada, 2017.

A lone wolf,
                 in his eyes smoke.
A single shooter,
                 in his eyes death
                         with his dice,
chance
chance
chance is an automatic weapon
a wolf of the desert
                 who studies the crowd
from the 32nd floor of the Mandalay Bay hotel,
security cameras show
his determination,
                 Nevada,
in his eyes the sand shines like broken
                 glass
the air whistles and helps breath fill
                 the lungs.

A man used to seeing luck spin
will now hold the fate of others,
only one who trusts the flame lives for the game,
who chases the flame even if it burns,
                       no matter how much it burns him,
security cameras show
the firmness of the pulse,
                 the slow
                     and unrelenting
                         step of death.

Stephen Paddock,
64 years old,

ya sujeta la suerte entre los dedos,
ya siente en la garganta un frío mineral,
la muerte es automática,
400 disparos por minuto,
400 oportunidades.

Alguien va a preguntarse las razones
del lobo solitario.

Ahora vuelan las almas,
las manos del azar son como el fuego,
                    su razón es la muerte,
400 razones por minuto
                    entre la multitud,
                              que grita,
                              que corre,
                              que se ahoga,
el miedo es automático,
el miedo es la certeza más insignificante,
más solitaria,
                    entre la multitud.

Las cámaras de seguridad muestran
el azar con sus lobos
                    hambrientos,
la muerte con sus dados,
la oscura soledad de los que corren
                    hacia ninguna parte.

holds luck between his fingers,
already feels a mineral cold in his throat,
death is automatic,
400 shots per minute,
400 opportunities.

Someone is going to ask the reasons
of the lone wolf.

Now the souls fly free,
the hands of chance are like fire,
                        their reason is death,
400 reasons per minute
                in the crowd,
                                that screams,
                                that runs,
                                that is choking,
fear is automatic,
fear is the most insignificant, most solitary
certainty
                in the crowd.

Security cameras show
chance with its wolves
                hungry,
death rolling its dice,
the dark solitude of those who run
                to nowhere.

First Baptist Church, Sutherland Springs, Texas, 2017.

Bienaventurados los que lloran,
porque ellos serán consolados.

Mateo, 5:4

Un hijo enfermo,
un hijo perseguido por la justicia,
un hijo que ya todo había malgastado,
un hijo blanco,
un tirador,
un hijo que entra al templo con hambre y sed,
esta es la sangre y el cuerpo del Señor,
pero fue a devorar el cuerpo de los otros,
bienaventurados los que lloran
bajo una lluvia de balas,
un joven blanco que conoce el sabor del infierno,
que ha probado el veneno,
va a llevarlo a la boca de los justos,
bienaventurados los que tienen hambre y sed de justicia,
pues ellos serán saciados
bajo una lluvia de plomo
hay cuatro ángeles atados en cada esquina del Éufrates,
no sopla viento alguno sobre la tierra de Sutherland Springs,
fuego,
azufre,
humo,
ha caído la gran Babilonia,
ha sido un hombre blanco,
un tirador,
bienaventurados los que lavan sus ropas
para tener derecho al árbol de la vida.

First Baptist Church, Sutherland Springs, Texas, 2017.

Blessed are they that mourn:
for they shall be comforted.

Matthew 5:4

A sick son,
a son pursued by justice,
a son who has already squandered everything,
a white son,
a shooter,
a son who enters the temple with hunger and thirst,
this is the body and blood of the Lord,
but he went to devour the bodies of others,
blessed are those who mourn
under a hail of bullets,
a young white man who knows the taste of hell,
who has tasted poison,
is going to take it to the mouths of the righteous,
blessed are those who hunger and thirst for righteousness,
for they will be satisfied
under a shower of lead
there are four angels tied at each corner of the Euphrates,
no wind blows on the land of Sutherland Springs,
fire,
brimstone,
smoke,
the great Babylon has fallen,
it was a white man,
a shooter,
blessed are those who wash their clothes
so as to have the right to the tree of life.

LA TIERRA SALVAJE

THE WILD LAND

El desdén y la serenidad de los mártires,
la madre de otro tiempo, condenada a muerte por bruja,
        quemada en la hoguera mientras sus hijos contemplan su
        martirio,
el esclavo perseguido que se detiene en su huida,
        se apoya en la cerca resoplando, bañado en sudor,
los dolores que le pinchan como agujas en las piernas y en el
        cuello, los disparos alevosos y las balas,
todo esto lo siento, todo esto soy.

The disdain and calmness of martyrs,
The mother of old, condemn'd for a witch, burnt with dry
        wood, her children gazing on,
The hounded slave that flags in the race, leans by the fence,
        blowing, cover'd with sweat,
The twinges that sting like needles his legs and neck, the
        murderous buckshot and the bullets,
All these I feel or am.

Walt Whitman, "Song of Myself"

El reverendo Martin Luther King Jr. avista la tierra prometida

4 de abril de 1968

Bendecidos aquellos que fueron a escucharte
porque fuiste la sangre fluyendo por la soledad.

La muerte,
agazapada entre la pobreza,
besó tu nombre desde el cañón de un rifle.

Precisamente a ti,
que subiste a la cima de la montaña,
que escuchaste los nombres de sus labios,
¿qué pueblo te esperaba
para alcanzar la tierra prometida?

¿Fueron los bosques de Birmingham, Alabama, lo que viste,
o una tierra partida por un río entre el este y el oeste?
¿Fueron los templos bombardeados
o tal vez un desierto insondable?

Los pobres de la tierra te reciben en sus bocas desdentadas,
tus cuatro hijos presienten el diluvio de tu bienaventuranza,
la noche silenciosa se ha llenado de perros que persiguen
los restos de los corazones
mientras arde otra casa,
America es ahora el fuego y la ceniza:
"ningún peligro frustrará a los amantes de este país".

Viste la tierra prometida y lo supiste,
jamás la alcanzarías
porque sólo una bala es suficiente para matar a un hombre,
un disparo preciso
y el cuerpo se desploma en la terraza del Motel Lorraine,

The Reverend Martin Luther King Jr. Sees the Promised Land

4 April 1968

Blessed are those who went to listen to you
because you were the blood flowing through their solitude.

Death,
crouched within poverty,
kissed your name from a rifle barrel.

You of all people,
who climbed to the top of the mountain,
who listened to the names from their lips,
what people awaited you
to reach the promised land?

Were the forests of Birmingham, Alabama, what you saw,
or a land divided by a river between east and west?
Were the temples bombed
or maybe an unfathomable desert?

The poor of the earth receive you with their toothless mouths,
your four children sense the ruins of your blessedness,
the silent night filled with dogs that devour
the remains of hearts
while another house burns,
America is now fire and ashes:
"No harm will come to those who love this country."

You saw the promised land and you knew
you would never reach it
because only one bullet is enough to kill a man,
a precise shot
and the body collapses on the terrace of the Lorraine Motel,

no alcanzará la tierra prometida pero sus ojos
vieron un día la gloria de la salvación.

Hay un hombre tendido sobre el suelo,
mirad, hay un cuerpo sin alma
un segundo después,
apenas existimos.

Ellos van a abrazarte, pero nadie sabría responder
quiénes son ellos,
aunque no queda duda de que son el futuro,
un futuro más grande que todo el pasado de la tierra.

Ya terminó, se acaba el espantoso viaje,
se escuchan las campanas,
reverendo,
todos los negros de Atlanta llegan a recibirte,
pero tú no respondes,
ya no te queda pulso ni voluntad,
alguien canta en tu nombre, alguien canta
mientras cierran
las puertas de la tierra sobre ti,
las puertas de la tierra prometida.

you will not reach the promised land but your eyes
they saw one day the glory of salvation.

There is a man lying on the ground,
look, there is a body without a soul
a second later,
we barely exist.

They are going to embrace you, but not one would know how to tell you
who they are,
although there is no doubt that they are the future,
a future greater than all the past of the earth.

It's over, the dreaded journey is over,
one can hear the bells,
Reverend,
all Black people of Atlanta come to receive you,
but you do not answer,
you have no pulse left or will,
someone sings in your name, someone sings
while they close
the doors of the earth upon you,
the doors of the promised land.

Gwendolyn A. T. borrada del paisaje del golfo de Mississippi

a Natasha Trethewey

Ya nunca estará sola porque su madre ha muerto

porque su cuerpo fue borrado
su voluntad
cautiva
del paisaje del golfo de Mississippi
en nombre de las buenas costumbres
que protegen la tierra
con leyes
con corrección
con títulos de propiedad

porque la muerte no deja sus huellas en la piedra
aunque devore el corazón

aunque llene de metralla los oídos con su llanto

y sus denuncias
por más que el odio sea

nuestra madre

nacida con la marca de la esclavitud

con el color
y el sexo
del golfo
de Mississippi

es preferible el silencio para cubrir su cuerpo sin vida

Gwendolyn A. T. Erased from the Mississippi Gulf Landscape

to Natasha Trethewey

She will never be alone because her mother has died

because her body was erased
her will
in the thrall
of the lands of the Mississippi Gulf
in the name of good practices
that protect this land
with laws
with correctness
with property titles

because death does not leave its footprints on the stone
even though it devours the heart

Even if death fills their ears with shrapnel with weeping

and its denunciations
no matter how much hate

our mother

born with the mark of slavery

with the color
and the sex
of the Mississippi's gulf

it is better to cover her lifeless body with silence

es preferible no escribir un nombre
en la lápida
porque los nombres
son también la huella de los otros

porque su nombre quedó escrito en un título de propiedad
como su cuerpo
nacida
bajo las leyes más elementales de los hombres
mujer
frente a las cruces ardientes
mujer
en el origen
del mundo

de rodillas

rincones encendidos
por la soledad

el ruido del agua sobre el porvenir
el olor de la tierra
los matorrales
el primer verano sin madre

un vacío
de oportunidades
robadas

en nombre de la justicia
y de la corrección.

Una mujer entra en la tierra del golfo
el silencio
y la piedra

it is better not to write a name
on the gravestone
because the names
are also the marks of the others

because her name was written on a property title
like your body
born
under the most elementary laws of men
woman

facing the burning crosses
woman
at the origin
of the world

on knees

hiding places lighted
by solitude

the sound of water over the future
the smell of the earth
the brush
the first summer without a mother

An empty space
of opportunities
stolen

in the name of justice
and of correctness

A woman enters the lands of the gulf
the silence
and the stone

la conocen
desde el origen del mundo.

have known her
from the origin of the world.

Eagle Pond: el pasado es un país bajo la tierra

a D.H.

he continues to daydream
that the past is a country under the ground
where the days practice their olds habits
over and over

Donald Hall

I

Él continúa imaginando,
espera
a que el invierno avance
y le cubra los miembros enfermos
con los brazos de los árboles desnudos,
su sombra es frágil como el recuerdo de una voz,
el invierno es anciano
y ya está cerca
de entrar en una larga noche.

Eagle Pond: The Past Is a Country under the Earth

to D.H.

he continues to daydream
that the past is a country under the ground
where the days practice their old habits
over and over

Donald Hall, "The Days"

I

He continues to dream,
he waits
as the winter comes
and covers his sickly limbs
with the arms of the bare trees,
his shadow is as fragile as the memory of a voice,
the winter is old
and it's already about
to enter a long night.

2

No ha cerrado los ojos.
Quería recordarla con los ojos abiertos,
para acercarla,
y ver.

2

He had not closed her eyes.
He wanted to remember her with her eyes open,
to bring her closer
and see.

3

No hay olor en la tierra.

Ya todo ha sido envuelto por la hora indecisa,
la que avanza despacio
en la espera,
la que separa el reencuentro con su oscuridad de grieta,
la misma que fue un día
maldita,
la hora suspendida para siempre en el aire,
el vértigo de un coche cayendo por un acantilado,
los minutos corriendo como liebres
frente a los cazadores
que disparaban desde todas partes,
seguros del final
como lo estaban todos.

3

The earth has no smell.

Everything has already been enveloped in the indecisive hour,
the one that advances slowly
in anticipation,
the one that separates the reunion from its crack in the darkness,
the same that was one day
cursed,
the hour suspended forever in the air,
the vertigo of a car falling over a cliff,
the minutes running like hares
before the hunters
that were shooting from everywhere,
certain of the end
as they all were.

4

Tiemblan sus dedos como los recuerdos
a punto de olvidarse.

No hay olor en la tierra
pero llueve
sobre la granja helada de Eagle Pond
llueve
sobre su propio pasado
llueve
    con agonía
el agua es incesante
     como el dolor
     como la espera
con todas sus preguntas
sobre la hora indecisa
     como el fondo marino
o la niebla callada
la granja de Eagle Pond
es un trozo de tiempo
     sumergido
en la laguna.

4

His fingers tremble like memories
about to be forgotten.

There is no smell of earth
but it is raining
on the cold farmhouse at Eagle Pond
it's raining
into his own past
it's raining
                in agony
the water incessant
                like suffering
                like waiting
with all its questions
concerning the indecisive hour
                like the seabed
or the silent fog
the Eagle Pond farm
is a moment in time
                submerged
in a lagoon.

5

Si el mar es la frontera de la tierra
la laguna es la herida
y en ella caben
todas las casas nuevas a punto de morir,
aquellas alcanzadas por la luz
y que son carne,
y que dan cobijo
a pájaros y a perros,
porque la soledad se exhibe en sus salones,
en sus muebles de roble,
bajo las chimeneas
donde el fuego encendido
ya no es lumbre,
sólo luz calurosa,
dentro de la laguna
duermen todas las casas que fueron destruidas,
es el invierno con su soledad,
con sus lentos minutos
y sus labios de incienso en las iglesias.

5

If the sea is the border of the earth
the lagoon is the wound
and in it fit
all the new houses about to die,
those reached by light
that are flesh,
and that give shelter
to birds and dogs,
because solitude is on display in the halls,
in the oak furniture,
under the chimneys
where the fire
is no longer fire,
only warm light,
within a lagoon
they sleep, all the houses that were destroyed,
it is winter with its solitude,
with your slow minutes
and her lips and the incense in the churches.

6

Cuando sale a buscarla,
temprano en la mañana,
abre la tierra, la tierra que está fría,
helada, de Eagle Pond,
cava
su propio agujero
sin darse por vencido,
sin que el cansancio o el cuerpo insuficiente
le lleven al desánimo,
afanosamente
remueve la tierra amontonada
porque allí están sus días más felices
y si cierra los ojos se imagina
como un hombre en el borde de aquella carretera,
la piedra siempre tiene un sabor fuerte,
también el alma,
el día es cada vez más largo,
cada vez más cansado
cava
como quien busca una casa
cava
tratando de regresar a Eagle Pond
para apagar la luz
y descansar los ojos
y salir del invierno.

6

When he goes out to look for her,
early in the morning,
he opens the earth, the ground that is cold,
frozen, at Eagle Pond,
he digs
his own hole
without giving up,
without letting fatigue or a weakened body
lead him to give up,
feverishly
he turns over the heaped earth
because these are his happiest days
and if he closes his eyes he imagines,
like a man on the edge of the road,
that the stone should have a strong taste,
also the soul,
the day is getting longer,
more and more weary
he digs
like someone looking for a house
he digs
trying to return to Eagle Pond
to turn off the light
and rest his eyes
and leave behind the winter.

Edgar Allan Poe es alcanzado en el puerto de Baltimore por las sombras que le persiguen

And the cloud that took the form
(When the rest of Heaven was blue)
Of a demon in my view—

"Alone"

Nunca dejaron de acompañarte.

Los perros desdeñosos
te hacían perder el equilibrio.

Tuviste que gritar,
blasfemias volcadas sobre las sombras
procurando apagar el escándalo de sus ladridos.

Otras veces
resultaba más recomendable hablar para tratar de calmarlos,
los susurros podían ser más convincentes
y detenerlos en cualquier esquina,
para después seguir caminando solo.

La soledad es un paseo por las calles de Baltimore.

Nunca pudiste liberarte,
aquellas sombras fueron creciendo,
como cuervos posados en las estatuas
con los ojos fijos en el vacío de un demonio que sueña.

A ti,
que estuviste en el filo de una lúgubre medianoche
viendo espectros de brasas moribundas reflejadas en el suelo.

Edgar Allan Poe Is Reached at the Baltimore Harbor by the Shadows That Pursue Him

> *And the cloud that took the form*
> *(When the rest of Heaven was blue)*
> *Of a demon in my view—*
>
> "Alone"

They always followed you.

Disdainful dogs,
they made you lose your balance.

You had to shout
blasphemies into shadows
trying to drown out the din of their barking.

Other times
it was advisable to talk and try to calm them,
whispers could be more convincing
and stop them on any corner,
so you could continue alone.

Solitude is a walk through the streets of Baltimore.

You could never free yourself,
those shadows were growing,
crows perched on the statues
with eyes fixed on the emptiness of a demon who dreams.

To you,
who were on the edge of a dismal midnight
watching specters of dying embers on the ground.

A ti,
que probaste el dolor,
que lo bebiste como un licor exquisito,
yo me acerco
y te miro tratando de buscarte al otro lado de la piedra
tallada por la desgracia,
del mismo modo que sucede con la belleza.

Nunca más sonarán las campanas de plata,
los barcos que ahora llegan al puerto de Baltimore
vienen llenos de gente demasiado asustada para hablar.

Traen una piedra en el sitio del corazón,
no intuyen estas sombras que deambulan por las calles,
estas sombras que no son ni hombres ni mujeres ni bestias,
acaso perros o pájaros o palabras en los picos de los pájaros
o en las mandíbulas.

Cuando pasan a su lado no son más que la brisa marina
de la que emergen.

Hay un silencio ahora
sobre el silencio
de las sombras.

Muerden como palabras
en el sitio del corazón.

To you,
who tasted sorrow,
who drank it like an exquisite liqueur,
I come close
and I look at you, trying to find you on the other side of the stone
carved by misfortune,
as happens with beauty.

Never again will the silver bells ring,
the ships that now arrive at the port of Baltimore
are filled with people too frightened to speak.

They bring a stone in place of the heart,
they do not sense these shadows that wander the streets,
these shadows that are not men or women or beasts
perhaps dogs or birds, or words in the beaks of the birds
or in their jaws.

When they pass they are nothing more than the sea breeze
from which they come.

There is a silence now
about silence
in the shadows.

They bite like words
in place of the heart.

Jack Kerouac busca una moneda para cruzar el último río de America

Veinticinco centavos
Times Square–Paterson
el viaje a pie es demasiado largo
la noche es más larga
esa colilla en el suelo es hermosa
todo lo hermoso es aplastado por la multitud
en esta ciudad
hay que levantar la cabeza
incluso después de trece mil kilómetros

Atravesada
America
el corazón profundo de America
en el que aprendí a sobrevivir
algunas veces con desesperación pero con la certeza
de que alguien pagaría la próxima comida
y de que siempre habría un hombro o un cuerpo sobre el que recostarse
y recibir calor
o placer
después de la intemperie
más densa y más vacía
veinticinco centavos
son el trayecto a casa
una
moneda
para cruzar el río
bajo la lengua
por el túnel Lincoln
una sola
moneda
miserables
hacia Nueva Jersey

Jack Kerouac Looks for a Coin to Cross the Last River of America

Twenty-five cents
Times Square–Paterson
the journey on foot is too long
the night is longer
that cigarette butt on the floor is beautiful
everything beautiful is crushed by the crowd
in this city
you have to raise your head
even after 13,000 kilometers

Crossing America
the buried heart of America
in which I learned to survive
sometimes with despair but with certainty
that someone would pay for the next meal
and that there would always be a shoulder or a body to lie on
and receive warmth
or pleasure
after the storm
twenty-five cents
for the ride home
a
coin
under the tongue
to cross the river
through the Lincoln Tunnel
a
coin
you miserable cheapskates
to New Jersey.

Kurt Cobain cierra la puerta de su invernadero

Me siento eufórico y triste,
voy a tomar algunas notas para una canción
si se acaban el asco y las ganas de vomitar.
Tengo un par de deseos cumplidos dentro de una caja de cigarros,
esta tristeza eufórica se parece a la música,
entra por todos los sentidos,
o tal vez sale, venosa, inyectable,
se dirige hacia otro que me observa
y me conoce
y se siente ofendido por mi indiferencia.

Ya había olvidado lo aburrida y estúpida que es la realidad
hay zumo de tomate en la nevera
voy a dejar alguna línea
hundiéndome
hundiéndome
el suelo está demasiado frío
guardo algunas canciones en una caja con forma de corazón
encontraré un lugar en el que el sol no me moleste.

Kurt Cobain Closes the Door of His Greenhouse

I feel euphoric and sad,
I'm going to take some notes for a song
if I can't get over the disgust and the desire to vomit.
I have a couple of wishes ready inside a cigar box,
this euphoric sadness is like music,
it enters through all my senses,
or maybe it comes out, venous, injectable,
directed toward another who observes me
and knows me
and feels offended by my indifference.

I had already forgotten how boring and stupid reality is
there's tomato juice in the fridge
I'm going to leave some lines behind
sinking
sinking
the floor is too cold
I've got some songs in a heart-shaped box
I will find a place where the sun doesn't bother me.

Jeff Buckley se adentra en las aguas del río Mississippi

Your faith was strong but you needed proof
You saw her bathing on the roof
Her beauty and the moonlight overthrew ya.

Leonard Cohen

Engendrado por el agua,
no son las fuentes del Nilo las que vienen a recibirte,
esta corriente es más fría,
fluye de norte a sur con vientos tempestuosos
crecidos en los glaciales y en los lagos.

Los ríos limpian, unen, purifican
pero también hay veces que los ríos
devienen animales hambrientos,
lobos escondidos bajo la piel del agua.

Memphis,
la luna está pidiendo quedarse
porque esta noche larga ha apagado sus luces
y ha cerrado los ojos sobre el río Mississippi.

Un hijo que ha aprendido del amor en sus calles,
un hijo que conoce el acorde secreto,
el cuarto, el quinto,
y después la caída;
va a adentrarse en el río
detrás de la belleza que una vez vio bañándose
sobre un tejado.

Pero va a llegar tarde.

Hallelujah.

Jeff Buckley Goes into the Waters of the Mississippi River

Your faith was strong but you needed proof
You saw her bathing on the roof
Her beauty and the moonlight overthrew ya.

Leonard Cohen

Sired by water—
it is not the headwaters of the Nile that come to receive you,
this current is colder,
flows from north to south with stormy winds
grown in the glaciers and in the lakes.

Rivers cleanse, unify, purify
but there are also times when rivers
become hungry animals,
wolves hidden under the water's skin.

Memphis,
the moon is asking to stay
because this long night has turned off its lights
and has closed its eyes on the Mississippi River.

A son who has learned about love in its streets,
a son who knows the secret chord,
the fourth, the fifth,
and then the fall,
will go into the river
following the beauty he once saw bathing
on a roof.

But he will be late.

Hallelujah.

Ya se cierran las aguas
cerca del puente,
el río ya está listo para mostrar sus fauces de lobo,
el Mississippi avanza
mientras un dios observa en las alturas
o en las profundidades
el último milagro de camino a la tierra prometida.

The waters are closing
near the bridge,
the river is ready to show its wolf jaws,
the Mississippi moves on
while a god watches in the heights
or in the depths
the last miracle on the way to the promised land.

El país de los lobos solitarios

*For the strength of the Pack is the Wolf, and the strength of the
Wolf is the Pack.*

Rudyard Kipling

Siempre hay un lobo en la noche del mundo
en las pesadillas de la tierra
bajo la luz de la luna
la ley
es un lobo
solitario
la ley es antigua
y cierta
como la noche
o como el ladrido de los perros
Lee Harvey Oswald muestra a la cámara su rifle de
        fabricación italiana
en el patio de su casa
a las afueras
porque la fuerza de la manada es el lobo
y porque siempre habrá un lobo solitario dispuesto a hacerle un favor
        a la patria
desde una ventana
o en un portal
o a quemarropa
lo importante es no devorarlo todo
hay que dejar la piel
o la cabeza
como dicen las leyes más elementales
James Earl Ray apunta con su rifle Remington al balcón del motel
        Lorraine en Memphis
bastará con una única dentellada
no es conveniente ser exagerado

The Country of Lone Wolves

*For the strength of the Pack is the Wolf, and the strength of the
Wolf is the Pack.*

Rudyard Kipling

There is always a wolf in the night of the world
in the nightmares of the earth
under the light of the moon
the law
is a wolf
lonely
the law is old
and certain
like the night
or like the barking of dogs
Lee Harvey Oswald shows the camera his Italian-made rifle
in the yard of his house
on the outskirts
because the strength of the pack is the wolf
and because there will always be a lone wolf willing to do the country
     a favor
from a window
or a doorway
or at point-blank range
the important thing is not to devour it whole
you have to leave the skin
or the head
as the most elementary laws say
James Earl Ray points his Remington rifle at the balcony of the
     Lorraine Motel in Memphis
a single bite will suffice
it is not advisable to lose control

como tampoco la soberbia
porque los lobos solitarios caminan para la manada
sobre la colina
o la nieve
o en el desierto
atravesando las pesadillas de la tierra
y las oraciones
Sirhan Bishara Sirhan vacía su revólver calibre 22
porque los lobos son nómadas que caminan en círculos
y cuando los invade una profunda tristeza
lloran
y su lamento atraviesa las llanuras y los bosques
donde alguien limpia sus huellas
mientras se lamen
desde la punta de la nariz hasta las patas
convencidos de su soledad
y de su desgracia
porque es el hambre quien los empuja
y el apetito su motivación
Mark David Chapman dispara un revólver calibre 38 especial
porque la guerra no se ha terminado
y los lobos caminan sobre el agua
y su idioma es la carne
y su guarida el mundo
y unos escapan con paso indiferente
mientras otros
              se detienen,
              seguros, paralizados,
sin atreverse a huir
sentados en un cine o en un portal
esperando el imperio de los hombres
y de la ley.

or be too proud
because lone wolves travel for the pack
over the hills
or the snow
or in the desert
crossing through the nightmares of the earth
and its prayers
Sirhan Bishara Sirhan empties his .22-caliber revolver
because wolves are nomads that walk in circles
and when a deep sorrow invades them
they cry
and their lament crosses the plains and forests
where someone erases their tracks
while they lick themselves
from the tip of the nose to the paws
firm in their solitude
and their misfortune
because it is hunger that pushes them
and appetite is their motivation
Mark David Chapman shoots a .38 Special revolver
because the war is not over
and the wolves walk on the water
and their language is flesh
and their lair the world
and some escape by walking away
while others
                    stop,
                    safe, paralyzed,
not daring to run
sitting in a movie theater or in a doorway
waiting for the empire of men
and law.

SOBRE EL AUTOR

Fernando Valverde nació en Granada (España) en 1980.

Cerca de 200 críticos de más de 100 universidades (Harvard, Oxford, Columbia o Princeton, entre ellas) lo eligieron el poeta más relevante en lengua española nacido después de 1970.

Entre sus libros de poemas destacan *Viento favorable*, *Madrugadas* o *Razones para huir de una ciudad con frío* (Visor). Con su libro *Los ojos del pelícano*, obtuvo el prestigioso Premio Emilio Alarcos del Principado de Asturias y se convirtió en el primer autor menor de treinta años con dos publicaciones en la editorial Visor. Entre los galardones que ha recibido destacan el Premio Federico García Lorca para universitarios españoles o sendos reconocimientos en el Premio Fray Luis de León y el Premio Juan Ramón Jiménez. *Los ojos del pelícano* ha sido publicado en Argentina, Colombia, México y Estados Unidos.

Su último libro, *La insistencia del daño* (Visor), ha ganado el 2014 Latino Literature Prize por el Latin American Writers Institute de la City University of New York. En 2014 fue nominado a un Premio Grammy por el disco *Jugar con fuego* con el cantaor Juan Pinilla. En la actualidad, trabaja como profesor de literatura en la University of Virginia en los Estados Unidos. Su poesía completa fue reunida en 2017 por Visor.

Twitter: @valverdefernan
Instagram: @fernandovalverdeoficial
Facebook: Fernando Valverde
Web: www.fernandovalverde.es

ABOUT THE AUTHOR

Fernando Valverde (born in Granada, Spain, in 1980) has been voted the most relevant Spanish-language poet born after 1970 by nearly two hundred critics and researchers from more than one hundred international universities (including Harvard, Oxford, Columbia, Princeton, Bologna, Salamanca, UNAM, and the Sorbonne). His books have been published widely in Europe and the Americas and translated into several languages. He has received significant awards for poetry in Spanish, among them the Federico García Lorca Poetry Prize, the Fray Luis de Léon Poetry Prize, and the Juan Ramón Jiménez Hispanic American Poetry Prize. His last book, *The Insistence of Harm*, was for months the best-selling book of poetry in Spain and received the 2014 Latino Literature Prize from the Latin American Writers Institute of the City University of New York. In 2014, his collaboration in a work of fusion between poetry and flamenco was nominated for a Latin Grammy. For ten years he has worked as a journalist for the Spanish newspaper *El País*. He directs the International Festival of Poetry in Granada, which has featured more than 300 authors, including several Nobel Prize laureates. In the United States, Valverde is a Visiting Distinguished Professor at the University of Virginia in Charlottesville.

Carolyn Forché's first volume of poetry, *Gathering the Tribes,* winner of the Yale Series of Young Poets Prize, was followed by *The Country Between Us, The Angel of History,* and *Blue Hour.* In March 2020, Penguin Press published her fifth collection of poems, *In the Lateness of the World,* a finalist for the Pulitzer Prize. She is also the author of the memoir *What You Have Heard Is True* (Penguin Press, 2019), a finalist for the National Book Award and winner of the Juan E. Méndez Book Award for Human Rights in Latin America. She has translated Mahmoud Darwish, Claribel Alegría, and Robert Desnos. Her international anthology *Against Forgetting* has been praised by Nelson Mandela as "itself a blow against tyranny, against prejudice, against injustice." In 1996 in Stockholm, she received the Edita and Ira Morris Hiroshima Foundation for Peace and Culture Award for her human rights advocacy and the preservation of memory and culture. She is one of the first poets to receive the Windham Campbell Prize from the Beinecke Rare Book and Manuscript Library at Yale University, and recently received a Lannan Literary Award for Poetry. She is a University Professor at Georgetown University in Washington, DC.

Copper Canyon Press is grateful to the Witter Bynner Foundation
for its support of this project.

Copper Canyon Press agradece a la Fundación Witter Bynner
por su apoyo a este proyecto.

Lannan Literary Selections

For two decades Lannan Foundation has supported the publication and distribution of exceptional literary works. Copper Canyon Press gratefully acknowledges their support.

LANNAN LITERARY SELECTIONS 2021

Shangyang Fang, *Burying the Mountain*

June Jordan, *The Essential June Jordan*

Laura Kasischke, *Lightning Falls in Love*

Arthur Sze, *The Glass Constellation: New and Collected Poems*

Fernando Valverde (translated by Carolyn Forché), *America*

RECENT LANNAN LITERARY SELECTIONS FROM COPPER CANYON PRESS

Mark Bibbins, *13th Balloon*

Sherwin Bitsui, *Dissolve*

Jericho Brown, *The Tradition*

Victoria Chang, *Obit*

Leila Chatti, *Deluge*

John Freeman, *Maps*

Jenny George, *The Dream of Reason*

Deborah Landau, *Soft Targets*

Rachel McKibbens, *blud*

Philip Metres, *Shrapnel Maps*

Aimee Nezhukumatathil, *Oceanic*

Camille Rankine, *Incorrect Merciful Impulses*

Paisley Rekdal, *Nightingale*

Natalie Scenters-Zapico, *Lima :: Limón*

Natalie Shapero, *Popular Longing*

Frank Stanford, *What About This: Collected Poems of Frank Stanford*

C.D. Wright, *Casting Deep Shade*

Matthew Zapruder, *Father's Day*

Poetry is vital to language and living. Since 1972, Copper Canyon Press has published extraordinary poetry from around the world to engage the imaginations and intellects of readers, writers, booksellers, librarians, teachers, students, and donors.

Copper Canyon Press gratefully acknowledges the kindness, patronage, and generous support of Jean Marie Lee, whose love and passionate appreciation of poetry has provided an everlasting benefit to our publishing program.

WE ARE GRATEFUL FOR THE MAJOR SUPPORT PROVIDED BY:

THE PAUL G. ALLEN
FAMILY FOUNDATION

CULTURE

Lannan

ART WORKS.

National Endowment for the Arts
arts.gov

A&
OFFICE OF ARTS & CULTURE
SEATTLE

WASHINGTON STATE
ARTS COMMISSION

TO LEARN MORE ABOUT UNDERWRITING
COPPER CANYON PRESS TITLES,
PLEASE CALL 360-385-4925 EXT. 103

WE ARE GRATEFUL FOR THE MAJOR SUPPORT PROVIDED BY:

Anonymous

Jill Baker and Jeffrey Bishop

Anne and Geoffrey Barker

In honor of Ida Bauer, Betsy
Gifford, and Beverly Sachar

Donna and Matthew Bellew

Will Blythe

John Branch

Diana Broze

John R. Cahill

Sarah Cavanaugh

The Beatrice R. and Joseph A.
Coleman Foundation

The Currie Family Fund

Stephanie Ellis-Smith and Douglas
Smith

Austin Evans

Saramel Evans

Mimi Gardner Gates

Gull Industries Inc. on behalf of
William True

The Trust of Warren A. Gummow

William R. Hearst, III

Carolyn and Robert Hedin

Bruce Kahn

Phil Kovacevich and Eric Wechsler

Lakeside Industries Inc. on behalf
of Jeanne Marie Lee

Maureen Lee and Mark Busto

Peter Lewis and Johnna Turiano

Ellie Mathews and Carl Youngmann
as The North Press

Larry Mawby and Lois Bahle

Hank and Liesel Meijer

Jack Nicholson

Gregg Orr

Petunia Charitable Fund and
adviser Elizabeth Hebert

Suzanne Rapp and Mark Hamilton

Adam and Lynn Rauch

Emily and Dan Raymond

Joseph C. Roberts

Jill and Bill Ruckelshaus

Cynthia Sears

Kim and Jeff Seely

Joan F. Woods

Barbara and Charles Wright

Caleb Young as C. Young Creative

The dedicated interns and
faithful volunteers of
Copper Canyon Press

The Chinese character for poetry is made up of two parts:
"word" and "temple." It also serves as pressmark for
Copper Canyon Press.

The poems are set in Adobe Caslon Pro.
Book design and composition by Phil Kovacevich.